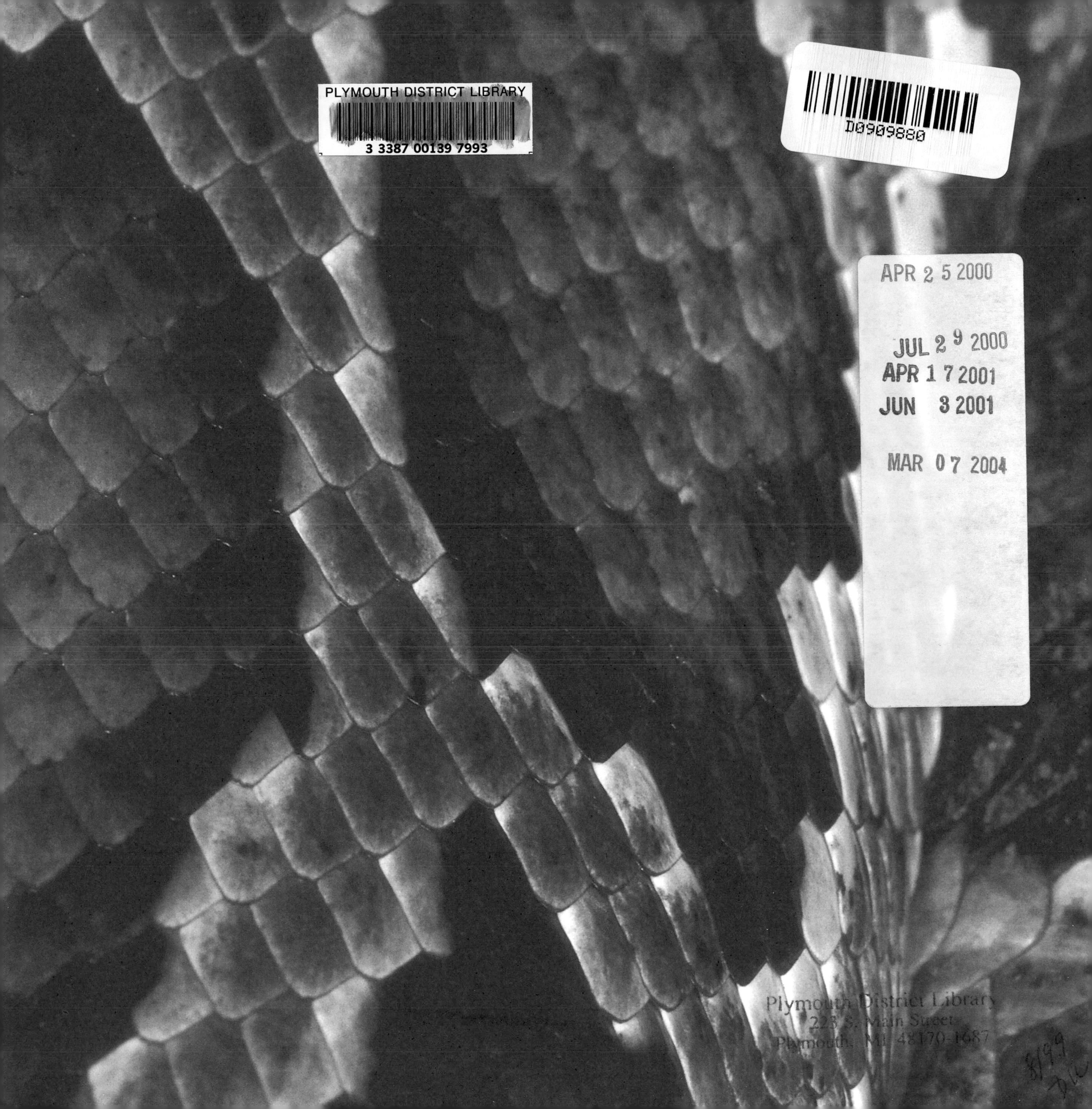

"A snake is the elegant product of a hundred million years of natural selection."
—Archie Carr, "In Praise of Snakes," 1971

SNAKES

Text by David Badger
Photographs by John Netherton

Voyageur Press

Edited by Gretchen Bratvold
Designed by Andrea Rud
Printed in Hong Kong
99 00 01 02 03 5 4 3 2 1

Library of Congress Cataloging-in-Publication Data
    Snakes / text by David Badger ; photography by John Netherton.
        p.   cm.
    Includes bibliographical references and index.
    ISBN 0-89658-408-9
    1. Snakes. 2. Snakes—Pictorial works. I. Netherton, John.
    II. Title.
    QL666.06B15   1999
    597.96—dc21   98-52379
                            CIP

Distributed in Canada by Raincoast Books, 8680 Cambie Street, Vancouver, B.C. V6P 6M9

Published by Voyageur Press, Inc.
123 North Second Street, P.O. Box 338, Stillwater, MN 55082 U.S.A.
651-430-2210, fax 651-430-2211

Educators, fundraisers, premium and gift buyers, publicists, and marketing managers: Looking for creative products and new sales ideas? Voyageur Press books are available at special discounts when purchased in quantities, and special editions can be created to your specifications. For details contact the marketing department at 800-888-9653.

On the frontispiece: *Green cat-eyed snake of Southeast Asia, also known as the green tree snake or cat snake.*
On the title pages: *At sunset, when male frogs begin calling from the waters, shores, and moss-draped cypress trees of Southern swamps, many snakes and other nocturnal predators that feed on amphibians become active. Lochloosa Lake, Florida.*
Inset on the title pages: *The mangrove snake is a handsomely patterned Asian species often glimpsed on branches overhanging water in mangrove swamps.*
Facing page: *Juvenile green tree python coils itself around a branch.*

Contents

Copperhead

Pigmy rattlesnake

Rough green snake

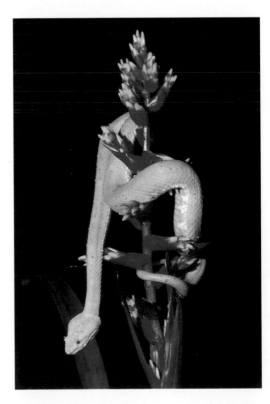

Eyelash viper

Dedication

For Sherry and Jeff, who tolerated my lengthy literary hibernation and welcomed my return to the real world. And for Hildy, who insured my regular excursions into the great out-of-doors.
—David Badger

For my sons, Jason, Joshua, and Erich.
—John Netherton

Acknowledgments

The author and photographer wish to express their gratitude to the following for their assistance with this book:

Brent Anderson; Eric Anderson; Scott Andrews; Mike Carlton; Mark Carroll; Jim Clark; Jamie R. Clark, director, U.S. Fish and Wildlife Service; Joseph T. Collins; Carrie Easley; Eastman Kodak; Nancy Gabriel; Jerry Gingerich; Shelly Graham; John Green; Harry Greene, University of California-Berkeley; Louis J. Guillette, University of Florida; Bill and Nancy Haast; Robert Henderson, Milwaukee Public Museum; Joseph Hewgley; Glenn Himebaugh; Rob Hoffman; Mark Kays; Howard Lawler; Greg Lepera; Betty McFall; Dale McGinnity, curator of reptiles, Nashville Zoo; Brian Miller, Department of Biology, Middle Tennessee State University; Joyce, Jacob, and Joshua Miller; Jason Netherton; Nikon Inc.; Alan Resetar, Field Museum of Natural History; Chris Richards; Richard Seigel, Southeastern Louisiana University; Sharon Smith; Gary Stolz; and Lex Thomas.

We are particularly indebted to Brian Miller for reviewing the manuscript and offering invaluable suggestions, as well as for his generous assistance in providing specimens to photograph.

Eyelash viper
Eyelash vipers of Central and South America commonly exhibit one of three color morphs: neon yellow, salmon pink, or lichen green. Wrapping their prehensile tail around a branch or vine, these venomous serpents will dangle in the air to strike at birds.

Introduction

Tiger rattlesnake
Facing page: *Americans have always been fascinated by rattlesnakes. Easterners featured rattlers on flags during the Revolutionary War, and Ben Franklin advocated making a rattlesnake the symbol of the United States. Today, visitors to Western and Southwestern states often hope to glimpse wild or captive rattlers such as this tiger rattlesnake, photographed in the Sonoran Desert near Tucson, Arizona.*

Rainbow boa
Inset: *A shimmering rainbowlike display of colors is visible when a Brazilian rainbow boa's iridescent scales catch the light.*

Benjamin Franklin was right: a snake would have made a splendid symbol of the United States of America. Old Ben never did approve of the bald eagle ("a Bird of bad moral Character," he groused), and though he touted the turkey ("a bird of Courage" and "a true original Native of America") from time to time, no one paid much attention. So in 1775, writing under the alias "An American Guesser," Franklin recommended the rattlesnake represent the United States.

"The Rattle-Snake is found in no other quarter of the world," Dr. Franklin wrote (incorrectly, it turns out); lacking eyelids, "she may therefore be esteemed an emblem of vigilance. She never begins an attack, nor, when once engaged, ever surrenders: She is therefore an emblem of magnanimity and true courage." Her weapons are "decisive and fatal," and her rattles total "just thirteen, exactly the number of the Colonies."

Just imagine, if the Continental Congress had seen fit to ratify Franklin's proposal, the community of snakes might have won the respect and admiration of the American people, perhaps even been safeguarded by the federal government. Instead, more than two centuries later, Americans still regard snakes with much the same fear and disgust they exhibited in Franklin's era, having closed their eyes to the extraordinary nature of these creatures.

Eastern indigo snake
The handsome and personable Eastern indigo snake is listed as threatened under the federal Endangered Species Act. Steady loss of habitat, overcollection by the pet trade, and poisoning from pesticides have caused a serious decline in indigo snake populations throughout Florida and southeastern Georgia.

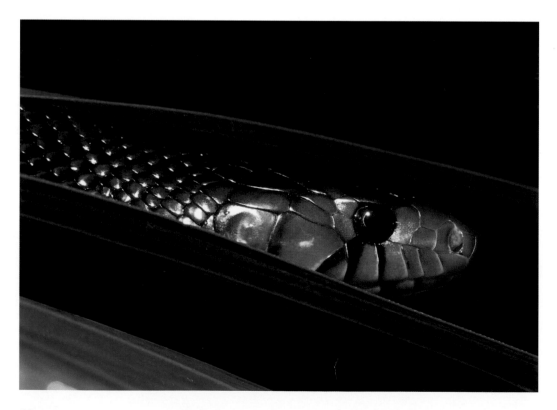

Quite by chance, my own eyes were opened thirty years ago by a smooth green snake I found while walking to school one day. When I showed the handsome serpent to my fourth-grade teacher, she immediately sensed a "learning opportunity" and offered to house it temporarily in a classroom terrarium. We admired that snake for weeks before reluctantly liberating it in a nearby park.

This serendipitous encounter with a suburban green snake, I now recognize, sparked my early interest in natural history. Further adventures with green snakes (ordered by mail from a snake farm in Louisiana) would ensue, followed by a science fair project involving venomous snakes (they were pickled, but that didn't prevent a local newspaper reporter from fainting when a fang accidentally impaled my partner's finger) and many summers as a nature counselor in Wisconsin.

A chance encounter with another green snake twenty years later—this one a photograph of a rough green snake in the Nashville *Tennessean*'s Sunday magazine—was to introduce me to the work of John Netherton. My efforts to obtain a print of this photograph ultimately led to many collaborations and a long-standing friendship.

At the time, I was teaching journalism at the University of Tennessee-Nashville, and John was working in the Department of Ophthalmology at the Vanderbilt University Medical Center, where he photographed patients' eyes. Human retinas and corneas did not excite John's passion, however, in the same way that snowy egrets, gray tree frogs, and Smoky Mountain waterfalls did, not to mention the occasional copperhead and water snake.

After John left Vanderbilt to conduct workshops and write and illustrate books, he began to devote more time to photographing wading birds, often taking pictures of amphibians and reptiles while waiting for his subjects to return to their nests. From time to time, I would edit a book for him, until 1994, when he invited me to write the text to accompany his breathtaking photographs for *Frogs* (Voyageur Press).

Two years later, when the publisher suggested we collaborate on a companion volume about snakes, I was hesitant. There were already plenty of books, I insisted, and to make my point I dragged John off to several bookstores and libraries. But John remained intrigued and argued that a volume similar to *Frogs* showcasing sharp-focus color photography alongside non-technical text might be an enticing introduction to snakes for readers of all ages. He invited me to examine his collection of reptile photographs, then snuck off to Florida to shoot some pictures of exotic specimens. When he returned, he had the photos to make his case: his new portraits of green tree pythons and emerald tree boas were spectacular, and I agreed to write the book.

From the start, we made it clear this would not be a field guide (Roger Conant and Joseph Collins' *Field Guide to the Reptiles and Amphibians of Eastern and Central North America* and Robert Stebbins' *Field Guide to Western Reptiles and Amphibians* are readily obtainable). Instead, we chose to focus on *representative* species, exotic and commonplace, from the United States and around the world. In the process, we came to showcase some of the more "ordinary" species frequently overshadowed by their more "charismatic" or glamorous cousins—in short, the very snakes that readers themselves might come across in their own backyards or while hiking in the woods.

To research the text, I immersed myself in herpetological literature dating back more than a century. Although scientific journals publish the bulk of researchers' findings today, I found myself repeatedly drawn to earlier books by Raymond L. Ditmars, Clifford H. Pope, Archie Carr, Carl Kauffeld, and Laurence Klauber, who were not only great naturalists and herpetologists but also great writers. I also discovered contemporary works by Richard Shine and Thomas Palmer, for example, that rank with the best by the aforementioned authors, along with authoritative studies by Carl Ernst, George Zug, Roger Barbour, Chris Mattison, Alan Tennant, Joseph Mitchell, and numerous other herpetologists. When Harry Greene, curator of herpetology at the University of California-Berkeley's Museum of Vertebrate Zoology, published his dazzling *Snakes: The Evolution of Mystery in Nature* midway through our undertaking, we were daunted but not routed.

During the course of my research, I was lured out of the library from time to time by a Middle Tennessee State University colleague, Brian Miller, who invited me to accompany him on several field trips with his herpetology students. Brian also managed to capture the elusive but essential green snake that appears in this volume—without which, I had only half-jokingly informed John, I would not write the book. Though recovering from a recent heart attack, John readily agreed to photograph this handsome snake, which reached his studio late one night by taxi.

One of our hopes for this book was to call attention to current threats to snake populations and their habitats. While collaborating on *Frogs*, we learned that many amphibian populations around the world are in jeopardy. Habitat destruction, pollution, pesticides, the pet trade, a deadly fungus, and damage from ultraviolet radiation entering the atmosphere through holes in the protective ozone layer are among the many causes of amphibian declines.

Since then, Americans have been shocked by reports of an epidemic of deformed frogs in thirty states and Canada, most likely the result of a pesticide found in lakes, ponds, and even well water, as well as stories of unprecedented die-offs of frogs in Central America. Many of these threats to our more "media-friendly" frogs pose an equal danger to snake populations, yet few people seem to know or care.

A century and a half ago, Henry David Thoreau bemoaned humans' "unnatural antipathy" toward snakes—the same ani-

Humans have exploited snakes for centuries—for their skins (made into articles of clothing), venoms (extracted for biomedical research and used to treat heart disease, nerve disorders, leukemia, and cancer), oils (used in liniments), and flesh (consumed widely throughout Asia and occasionally in upscale U.S. restaurants).

Reptiles are the fastest-growing area of the pet trade.

mosity visible today. Sadly, most people would rather bludgeon a snake than become acquainted with one. But for snakes, just as for frogs, time is running out: unless serious efforts are made to heighten public awareness of threats to snake populations and their habitats, we will face extinctions in the new millennium.

In the early 1950s, Florida herpetologist Archie Carr declared that Americans must make the case that reptiles should be saved. "Only then," he said, "are you ready for the harder jobs, like justifying a future for snakes, which have no legs, hear no music, and badly clutter subdivisions."

Justifying any animal's existence shouldn't be necessary in this era of heightened environmental consciousness, but, in the case of snakes, it appears essential. Although the economic value of snakes cannot be precisely calculated, even the most cold-blooded capitalist must concede the devastating impact that rats and mice would have on the world's grain supplies if unchecked by serpents. By destroying these pests, snakes also play an important role in controlling diseases transmittable to humans.

Of course, man has been exploiting snakes for centuries—for their skins (made into articles of clothing), venoms (extracted for biomedical research and used to treat heart disease, nerve disorders, leukemia, and cancer), oils (used in liniments), and flesh (consumed widely throughout Asia and occasionally in upscale U.S. restaurants).

Snakes may not command the high profile frogs do, but there's no mistaking their grip on the human imagination. Athletic teams, music groups, and entertainers are named after snakes, as are aircraft, automobiles, and ships. Fox snakes, green snakes, pythons, and rattlesnakes have appeared in advertisements for everything from women's apparel and men's ties to computers and French perfume. Clothing boutiques feature python-skin patterns on women's tanksuits, and images of snakes appear on many forms of jewelry (Queen Victoria wore a gold snake engagement ring and diamond snake bracelet). Tattoos with snakes are popular (former *Washington Post* executive editor Ben Bradlee has one on his right buttock), as are snake toys, T-shirts, mugs, calendars, and other paraphernalia.

Today, pet snakes are not only prized, they're fashionable, and the American Federation of Herpetoculturists reports that reptiles are the fastest-growing area of the pet trade. But some hobbyists live dangerously as well as in defiance of state or local laws. ("Keeping a venomous snake in your home is like keeping a loaded and cocked handgun in your china cabinet," Carl Ernst and George Zug warn. "Sooner or later, someone will be seriously, perhaps even fatally, injured.") In 1996 an Egyptian cobra escaped from a backyard in Stoneham, Massachusetts, only to turn up several months later in a fourth-grade classroom, where a youngster discovered it behind a recycling bin.

Aesthetically, snakes are among the most beautiful creatures on earth. "Though alligators, snakes, etc., naturally repel us, they are not mysterious evils," naturalist John Muir observed after his thousand-mile walk to the Gulf of Mexico in 1867. "They dwell happily in these flowery wilds, are part of God's family, unfallen, undepraved, and cared for with the same species of tenderness and love as is bestowed on angels in heaven or saints on earth."

Red-tailed green rat snake
The red-tailed green rat snake is an arboreal species found in mangrove and bamboo forests of Southeast Asia and the Philippines. This handsome though aggressive serpent has a long snout, beautiful green scales, and a reddish-brown tail.

Undoubtedly, fear of venomous snakes motivates human animosity toward all snakes and is responsible for mankind's efforts to extinguish snake populations in all corners of the world. One way to counter this widespread human hatred is to dispel unfounded myths and portray snakes with greater tolerance and sensitivity. As Marjorie Kinnan Rawlings, author of *The Yearling*, once observed, "It is difficult to be afraid of anything about which enough is known."

Years ago, many herpetologists wrote popular books about reptiles that were steeped in vivid descriptions and colorful anecdotes; today, such natural histories are less common and not always appreciated by academics. Ironically, these classic works are invaluable aids for encouraging new generations to appreciate the herpetofauna around them.

"The naturalists are dying off and have few heirs," writes Reed Noss, editor of *Conservation Biology*. "Will the memoirs of future biologists contain vibrant descriptions of childhoods spent crawling through swamps and grabbing snakes? . . . Somehow I do not think that stories of boyhoods and girlhoods spent playing Nintendo and watching *Teenage Mutant Ninja Turtles* will be nearly so enthralling."

All forms of mass communication—from newspapers and magazines, scientific journals, and natural history books to motion pictures, radio, television, and the Internet—can enhance our understanding and appreciation of our planet's animal life. With any luck, every individual whose eyes are opened and whose interest is engaged will become a recruit in the defense of the environment. Which, it goes without saying, includes snakes.

> "Snakes have been classified, dissected, and explained in terms of evolution and ecology. Their scales and teeth have been counted; their venoms detoxified, chromatographed and fractionated. Yet with all this, the snake remains today the one animal that man universally respects and fears, covertly loves and intensely hates."
> —Sherman and Madge Minton, *Venomous Reptiles*, 1969

Chapter 1

Snakes and Humans

King cobra

Facing page: *The sight of a venomous king cobra from tropical Asia spreading its hood and rearing its head strikes fear into the hearts of many humans. Zookeepers believe this cobra is the most intelligent of all snakes, and some specimens apparently recognize and anticipate the arrival of their keepers, while displaying hostility toward strangers.*

Rattlesnake billboard, Akela Flats, New Mexico

Inset: *Rattlesnakes have suffered at the hands of humans for centuries. Their rattles, skin, flesh, and fangs are still exploited in the American Southwest for numerous products and curios, including earrings, wallets, hatbands, canned rattlesnake meat, and snake-oil liniment.*

It was a warm summer day in 1939, and the city of London was abuzz with talk of impending war. Suddenly, an air-raid siren—the first of World War II—shattered the composure of the city. Acting on the order of the British cabinet, the head keeper of the Reptile House at the London Zoo set off to do his duty: assisted by his staff, he decapitated every venomous serpent on the premises, including his favorite, a magnificent female king cobra.

"It was sickening," the keeper recalled years later. "There we were, choppin' away hour after hour, choppin' the heads off thousands of pounds' worth of valuable venomous reptiles." Devastated by the mass execution, he and his associates shed tears afterward—especially when they learned the siren had been a false alarm.

"All the poisonous snakes and poisonous insects at the Zoo have now been destroyed," *The Times* dutifully reported the next day. "For the first time in the history of the Zoo, we have no poisonous animals here."

The cabinet, it turns out, had feared panic would break out if Hitler's Luftwaffe dropped bombs on Regent's Park and liberated the zoo's most infamous animals. Other beasts, however, including the elephants, giant pandas, and rare zebras, were evacuated to the Zoological Society's country estate.

But the damage was done, and the message was clear: serpents would not be allowed to terrorize the citizens of London. Not for the first time, fear of snakes would account for disproportionate acts of cruelty.

"We regard serpents with a destructive hatred purely and simply because we are taught so from childhood," author W. H. Hudson asserted in 1919. "Show a child by your gestures and actions that a thing is fearful to you, and he will fear it; that you hate it, and he will catch your hatred."

Why is it that, of all the earth's creatures, snakes inspire such universal fear and loathing? The answer lies in the human race's troubled history with its reptilian "adversaries"—a history that dates back thousands of years and reaches a turning point in Hebrew and Christian accounts of the Garden of Eden.

Humans and serpents co-exist in virtually every corner of the world, and, where the serpents are venomous, humans have learned to beware the fangs that inflict pain and death. Yet, despite a strong survival instinct, humans have also demonstrated an intense fascination with snakes—a curiosity about these mysterious creatures that propel themselves across desert sands, through fields of grain, and into the green drapery of the rain forest without benefit of arms or legs. Like other unusual animals, serpents have come to figure in the myths and rituals of many cultures—venerated by some, despised by others.

In ancient Sumerian mythology (c. 3000 B.C.), King Gilgamesh chops down the Huluppu tree for the goddess of love in a garden guarded by a snake. In a later Babylonian poem, the *Epic of Gilgamesh* (c. 2000 B.C.), the king dives to the bottom of the sea to retrieve a plant that offers eternal life. On the journey home, however, a serpent appears and steals the magical Plant of Life. After tasting it, the snake promptly sheds its skin and is rejuvenated, whereupon Gilgamesh resigns himself to his fate and returns home to die.

The Babylonian Plant of Life reappears in Hebrew and Christian traditions as the Tree of Knowledge of Good and Evil. In the Old Testament Book of Genesis, a serpent "more subtle than any other wild creature that the Lord God had made" entices Eve to taste the forbidden fruit of a tree "in the midst of the garden"; after she shares the fruit with Adam, "the eyes of both were opened." An angry God then lays a curse on the serpent: "Upon your belly you shall go, and dust you shall eat all the days of your life."

Apparently, serpents had an upright shape before the Fall and must have possessed vocal cords as well. Early rabbis, Marilyn Nissenson and Susan Jonas report in their book *Snake Charm*, concluded that "while other animals could talk with each other in animal language, only the snake knew Hebrew. In punishment after the Fall, the serpent's tongue was split and all it could do was hiss."

In the aftermath, the evil reputation of the biblical serpent was to exert a powerful impact on human perceptions of the real animal.

During the Middle Ages, according to some scholars, the Christian notion of the serpent as Satan took hold when artists' renditions of the Fall began to change. "Before the twelfth century," Nissenson and Jonas state, "scenes of the Temptation showed three figures: a snake wrapped around the tree, Adam, and Eve. As the

Humans and serpents have co-existed in virtually every corner of the world.

devil emerged as a more active player, the drama shifted to the tension between the snake and Eve . . . [and] the snake began to acquire a human face." Several centuries later, John Milton would reinforce this image in his epic poem *Paradise Lost*.

For the early Hebrews, however, it was the serpent—long associated in Near Eastern religions with fertility and death—and not Satan who tempted Eve. The serpent was already a symbol of evil, since it was worshipped by the Hebrews' enemies, the Egyptians. Snakes were venerated in Egypt as kin to the gods, and a dozen deities, including the cobra goddess Neith, founder of the universe, were represented by snakes. Egyptians also equated snakes with fertility, and, fittingly, the spirit of the River Nile was a snake god. Gold jewelry prominently featured cobras with their hoods spread, and King Tutankhamen and other royalty were entombed with these amulets to protect them from venomous bites in the afterlife.

In the Old Testament, Moses—himself a highly respected snake shaman—leads the Hebrews on their exodus from Egypt, during which God sends swarms of fiery serpents to plague those who murmur against him. When the compassionate Moses prays for assistance, he is told to erect a pole bearing a serpent, and this bronze serpent later becomes his trademark. Eight hundred years later, King Hezekiah shatters the bronze serpent made by Moses, angered that the people of Israel have come to idolize it. In later centuries, Christians would continue to distance themselves from the cult of ophiolatry (snake worship) and shun serpents for their role in the fall of man and their association with their Egyptian enemies.

The Greeks and Romans too emphasized serpents in their cultures. Apollo, the Greek god of sunlight and prophecy, killed a python as a youth and later established the python as the sacred guardian of the Delphic Oracle. Aesculapius, the Greco-Roman god of healing, created a personal totem from two snakes entwined around a staff; called a caduceus, this device became the symbol of the medical profession. In the Roman Empire, snakes were believed to bring good luck. The Romans built shrines to serpents, encouraged them to take up residence in their homes and public places, and incorporated snakes into numerous myths appropriated from the Greeks.

Serpents appear widely throughout the history and folklore of other cultures as well. When Alexander the Great invaded India, he found that maharajahs kept cobras as totems. According to Hindu legend, the deity Shesha coiled its huge body around the earth to safeguard it from evil forces. The Hindu god Siva, renowned for his reproductive powers, is venerated as the king of serpents, and religious shrines throughout India depict snakes entwined around Siva. Residents of some Indian cities set aside one corner of their garden for cobras, which were believed to be descendants of the serpent gods. According to nineteenth-century historian H. J. Rivatt-Carnac, pictures of snakes were delivered in the manner of valentines during an Indian festival called the Naga panchami.

In ancient China and Japan, serpents were often equated with dragons, and Japanese volcanoes were said to be guarded by supernatural serpents. Philippine tribal legends told of "weresnakes" similar to European werewolves, and in Australia, Ab-

Stuffed rattlesnake

Stuffed rattlesnakes and an array of other items, such as snakeskin boots, lamp shades, and paperweights with rattler heads, are sold at truck stops throughout the Southwest. Many trophy snakes collected in Texas and Oklahoma during annual "rattlesnake roundups" are slaughtered for these products.

"How sharper than a serpent's tooth it is To have a thankless child!" —William Shakespeare, "King Lear"

Native Americans created in Wisconsin and Ohio ancient monuments in the shape of giant open-jawed serpents, some of which stretch as long as 700 feet (213 m).

origines believed the Rainbow Serpent appeared in the sky during the rainy season. In West Africa, the python god Danh-gbi was venerated in Dahomey (now Benin), where molesting a python invited severe punishment. During the eighteenth and nineteenth centuries, European intruders caught viewing secret Danh-gbi ceremonies risked death.

Giant 300-foot (91.44 m) serpent mounds have been discovered in Scotland, and at Rouffignac, in central France, an underground cave features designs of entwined serpents on its ceiling's Dome of Serpents. In Italy, the village of Cocullo commemorates St. Dominic's expulsion of a plague of vipers in 1218 with an annual parade featuring a statue of the saint draped with live snakes.

The citizens of Ireland proudly boast that their patron saint, Saint Patrick, banished all the serpents from their country with his prayers and holy benedictions. Their claim that no native snakes inhabit their isle is correct; scientists have concluded, however, that glaciers had more to do with the absence of snakes than did Ireland's great benefactor. As the climate warmed and the ice sheets melted, animals began migrating across the land link between continental Europe and the British Isles, but reptiles did not migrate until later, by which time the link had been submerged by glacial meltwater.

In the Americas, early emperors boasted they descended from serpents, and the pre-Columbian serpent god Quetzalcoatl was a composite of two native animals: the rattlesnake and the quetzal, a native bird with brilliant green and gold plumage. When the Spanish conqueror Hernando Cortés marched against the Aztec capital in 1519, he was welcomed by Montezuma, who believed Cortés to be a descendant of this god.

Across North America, native tribes wove their own rich tapestry of legends involving snakes. In Wisconsin and Ohio, Native Americans left behind ancient monuments in the shape of giant open-jawed serpents, some of which stretch as long as 700 feet (213 m). Many traditions revolve around the rattlesnake (sometimes called the "great father"), perhaps the best known of which is the Hopi snake dance. Former President Theodore Roosevelt, who was invited to watch the Hopi snake priests prepare for a ceremony, later wrote that the snakes were dipped into water and "hurled" across the room to the altar, where they "woke to an interest in life." At sundown, the snakes were sprinkled with sacred cornmeal, then seized by the dancers and carried in their mouths; after the dance, the priests would dash in all four directions of the compass and release the snakes out of sight. Roosevelt suspected that the rattlers' venom had been milked or their fangs extracted, and decades later this was confirmed by herpetologists.

To the early white settlers of North America, the abundance of snakes was disconcerting, especially the venomous rattlesnakes. Botanist John Bartram, a friend of Ben Franklin, "was born into a world at war against snakes," biographer Thomas Slaughter notes. "The warfare was total; no prisoners were taken and ranks were assigned. . . . Whacking a rattler was something of a male rite of passage in colonial America—a moral obligation, a public service, and dangerous fun all in one." Bartram's son, William, who became America's first great natural historian, learned from his father that "the beauty of the living serpent was superior to that of the dead" and argued forcefully throughout his lifetime that the lives of these creatures should be spared.

Although Thomas Jefferson never shared his friend Franklin's enthusiasm for the rattlesnake, the president did express interest in an account by Meriwether Lewis regarding the medical use of rattlesnake rattles during his expedition to the Pacific. When Sacagawea, the pregnant young Indian wife of one of his men, went into painful and protracted labor, she was administered two rings of a rattle "broken in small pieces and added to a small quantity of water," Lewis wrote. "Whether this medicine was truly the cause or not I shall not undertake to determine, but I was informed that she had not taken it more than ten minutes before she brought forth."

Americans who followed in Lewis and Clark's footsteps encountered many unusual snakes and concocted wild tales to account for the snakes' behavior. In the best known of these stories, serpents rolled up into hoops, swallowed their young, milked cows, blew poisonous breath onto their victims, and charmed their prey. Some storytellers boasted they knew "sure cures" for rattlesnake bites, Laurence Klauber recalls, including application or consumption of toads, rabbits, skunks, live split chickens, milk, cheese, snakeweed, onions, garlic, turpentine, kerosene, crocodile teeth, and powdered human teeth. "On occasion," Klauber adds, "the victim was buried to his neck in a manure pile."

In New Orleans, voodoo-practicing slaves transported from Haiti and Africa brought with them a snake-worshipping cult that engaged in feverish dances and animal sacrifices. "Dr. John" and Marie Laveau, the king and queen of the voodoo sect, achieved fame for a rite in which the queen would lie on a box containing a snake and begin writhing when the spirit of the snake possessed her. Eventually, officials felt compelled to banish the voodoo snake-worshipers from the city.

In Tennessee, George Went Hensley introduced snake handling to his rural congregation in 1909 after pondering a biblical verse that read: "In my name . . . they shall take up serpents" (Mark 16:17–18). Hensley encouraged his communicants to reach into a box of copperheads and timber rattlesnakes and remove one as a test of faith. Eventually, he was forced to move to Kentucky, and later Florida, after a number of his followers died from snakebites. Hensley himself survived more than 400 bites but died from the venom of an Eastern diamondback in 1955.

"To date, at least seventy-one people have been killed by poisonous snakes during religious services in the United States," reporter-author Dennis Covington wrote in 1995. (Two more victims have died since then after being bitten during church services in Kentucky and Alabama.) Handling "isn't a parlor trick," Covington explains; "the rattlesnakes haven't been tampered with or defanged."

In numerous societies, ancient and modern, the serpent has been a symbol of the male organ. "So ubiquitous is the phallus-snake," anthropologist Weston La Barre asserts, "indeed the question might be phrased, Where is the snake *not* a phallic symbol?" Psychologist Sigmund Freud claims that, of the many animals that appear in dreams, snakes are "above all the most important symbols of the male organ."

As instruments of horror and death, snakes are frequently employed in literature and film. In the Sherlock Holmes tale

*R*eligious snake-handling pioneer George Went Hensley encouraged his communicants to reach into a box of copperheads and timber rattlesnakes and remove one as a test of faith. Hensley survived more than 400 bites but died from the venom of an Eastern diamondback in 1955.

"The Speckled Band," for example, the villain employs a Russell's viper to murder a foe. In Oliver Wendell Holmes' 1861 novel *Elsie Venner*, the mother of the title character is bitten by a timber rattlesnake prior to giving birth; in the years that follow, her daughter is seized by convulsions, rattles castanets, "undulates" her lithe body, and, with "diamond eyes glittering," flings herself "in a coil" to the floor.

One of the best-known snake stories is Rudyard Kipling's "Rikki-Tikki-Tavi," from *The Jungle Book*, about a loyal mongoose that defends a family from a pair of vicious cobras. More recent works of fiction, such as Max Phillips' *Snakebite Sonnet*, Bard Young's *The Snake of God,* and Tim McLaurin's *The Last Great Snake Show*, attest to the popularity of serpents in literature. (For good measure, Tom Wolfe names a law firm Crotalus, Adder, Cobra, and Krait in his novella *Ambush at Fort Bragg*.)

Children's literature is filled with snake tales as well, including Trinka Noble's *The Day Jimmy's Boa Ate the Wash* (and its two sequels), Tomi Ungerer's *Crictor,* Brian Wildsmith's *Python's Party,* and Janell Cannon's *Verdi*. In popular music, too, snakes show up regularly as the subject of folksongs, Broadway tunes, and country hits.

At the movies, snakes have made many memorable appearances, and some have even been the star. In *Sssssss,* a deranged university professor devises a way to turn humans into snakes with cobra venom; in *Stanley,* a Vietnam vet and his rattlesnake wreak vengeance on unscrupulous business associates; and in *Anaconda,* snake hunter Jon Voight encounters a monstrous constrictor in the Amazon with a ravenous appetite for humans.

As pets, snakes have always been popular, even taking up residence in the White House during the presidency of Theodore Roosevelt. Son Quentin once deposited a large kingsnake and "two wee snakes" in the president's lap while he was conducting business with the attorney general. The president then suggested Quentin take his pets into the next room, "where four Congressmen were drearily waiting. . . . I thought he and his snakes would probably enliven their waiting time."

Today, herpetoculturists around the world collect and breed snakes, host reptile expos in major cities, and share information, veterinary advice, and "baby photos" of their pets on the World Wide Web, where several hundred websites are devoted to reptiles. Museums, zoos, universities, and environmental organizations also post invaluable scientific data on their home pages.

Snakes, it would seem, are everywhere—even as their ranks are being systematically reduced. Wart snakes, wolf snakes, dog-toothed cat snakes, stink snakes, litter snakes, thirst snakes, stiletto snakes, coffee snakes, Halloween snakes, tommygoffs, bandy-bandys, and wutus—their names conjure up all manner of fantasies, phobias, dreams, and fears. Most of which are hard to dislodge, even with the facts.

As of 1995, at least seventy-one people have been killed by poisonous snakes during religious services in the United States.

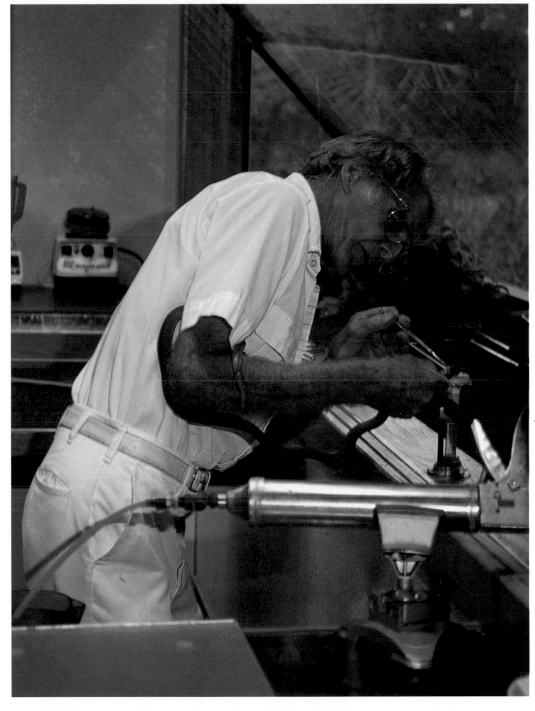

Bill Haast milking a venomous snake

At his laboratory in southern Florida, herpetologist Bill Haast extracts venom from a green mamba for use in the manufacture of antivenom to treat snakebite. Scientists have discovered that some snake venoms are also effective in treatment of heart disease, cancer, leukemia, and other illnesses.

Physical Characteristics and Behavior

Asian vine snake
Facing page: *Some snakes are short and stocky, while others, such as the Asian vine snake, are long and slender. Stretched out motionless on a vine or bamboo branch, this well-camouflaged serpent will extend its tongue for fifteen to twenty seconds at a time, perhaps to attract prey.*

Copperhead
Inset: *The five subspecies of copperheads account for a large share of the venomous snakebites reported in the United States.*

Shape and Size

"Most people know what a snake looks like: a sort of eel or worm covered in scales," remarks natural history writer Thomas Palmer. "A lot of people," he adds, "don't want to know any more."

Sad but true. Not one of Palmer's unfortunate trio—eels, worms, and snakes—inspires much love or affection; in fact, the scorn heaped upon all three is probably surpassed only by fanatical fear and loathing.

Yet just because snakes and other long, limbless creatures slither or swim without benefit of legs doesn't mean they're unworthy of our understanding and appreciation. In fact, snakes have adapted so very well to life on this planet that it would be downright perverse to argue that a creature that burrows in the earth, glides across it, swims the waters, climbs the trees, and "flies" from the forest canopy is biologically inferior to its brethren because of the design of its body.

Snakes are the "elegant product" of millions of years of natural selection, Archie Carr once observed. Most are perceived to be cylindrical (rounded in cross section), yet many are somewhat squarish or shaped like a bread loaf. Whether the snake's long, streamlined torso evolved from burrowing lizards (as has long been supposed) or from aquatic ancestors (as recently re-evaluated fossil evidence now suggests), its general shape provides marvelous flexibility in adapting to a wide range of environmental conditions and habitats. Vine, tree, and twig snakes are very slender, with long, prehensile tails. On the other hand, burrowing snakes have relatively stocky bodies, and aquatic species, such as the sea snakes, generally have flattened bodies and oarlike tails.

Some species, such as the Asian vine snake, have narrow, pointed snouts and slender tails, while others, such as blind snakes, have blunt heads and tails. Among Madagascan vine snakes, the female has a broad, leaflike appendage on her snout and the male a scooped, pointed spike, while the tentacled snake of Southeast Asia sports a pair of cigar-shaped protuberances that may actually be feelers.

Yet there is even greater disparity in size than in shape. Ranging from the tiny thread snakes, blind snakes, and worm snakes—some adults are as small as 4⅜ inches (11.1 cm)—to the imposing reticulated pythons and anacondas, which allegedly reach 30 feet (9 m) or more, snakes excite the imagination of humans because, as Clifford H. Pope once pointed out, "the larger a snake, the more dangerous it appears to be."

Reports of truly "giant" snakes turn up in numerous accounts by nineteenth- and early twentieth-century explorers. According to Bernard Heuvelmans, who at-

tempted to locate the longest snake on record, a nearly 75-foot (23 m) anaconda was reportedly sighted in 1947 on the Rio das Mortes (River of Death) in South America. Lacking a measuring instrument, members of the expedition took a piece of string, marked off a length from the tip of one man's fingers to his opposite shoulder, and measured the reptile several times. Each time, the anaconda came out at twenty-four or twenty-five lengths of the piece of string.

"I had heard so many tales of giant snakes," one witness said later, "that I supposed the whole of the Amazon was crawling with monsters of this size." But members of the expedition had no proof to offer later.

"We should have liked to take the snake's skin back," confessed the witness, "but we had neither the time to skin the beast nor to prepare its hide. . . . Think what a piece of skin more than 60 feet [18 m] long by 4 feet 6 inches [1.37 m] wide would have weighed! We should have had our work cut out to carry it—or for that matter the head. Besides, who would have been crazy enough to lug a piece of rotting meat on his back in that heat through country infested with insects?"

Despite this and other accounts of monster anacondas and boas (not to mention the 40-foot [12 m] whopper in the film *Anaconda*), scientists have been unable to confirm with confidence any reports of snakes longer than 30 feet (9 m).

Half a century ago, the New York Zoological Society posted a $5,000 reward for any living specimen over 30 feet; more recently, the Wildlife Conservation Society has posted a $50,000 reward for any specimen 30 feet or longer. So far, there have been no takers.

Yet the rumors persist. As recently as

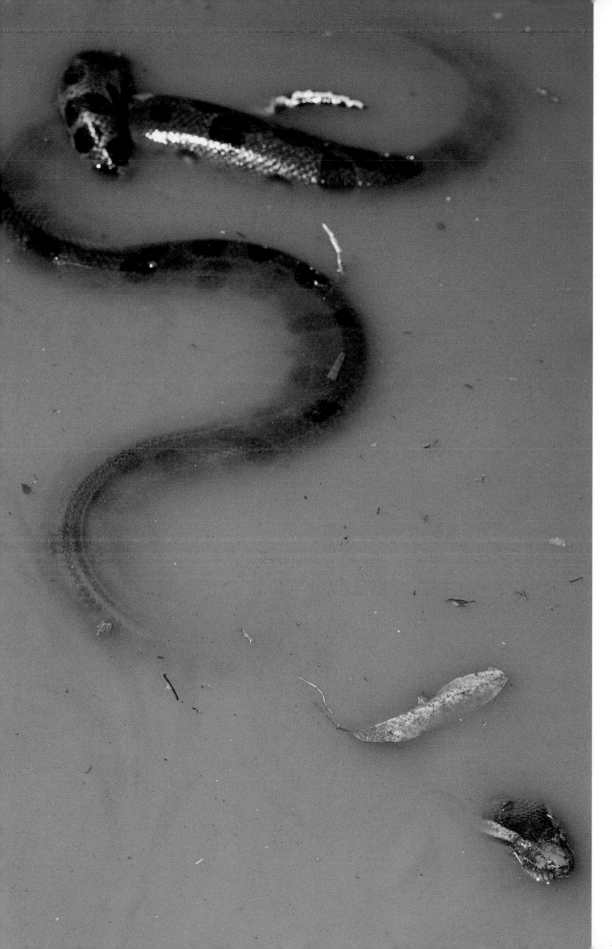

> "The long, limbless body, lithely and mysteriously gliding on the surface; the glittering scales and curious mottlings, bright or lurid; the statuesque, arrowy head, sharp-cut and immovable; the round lidless eyes, fixed and brilliant; and the long, bifurcated tongue, shining black or crimson, with its fantastic flickering play before the close-shut, lipless mouth—that is the serpent."
> —W. H. Hudson,
> *The Book of a Naturalist*, 1919

Green anaconda

The anacondas of tropical South America are reputed to be the world's longest snakes, reaching lengths of nearly 30 feet (9 m). These giant snakes, which can weigh up to 400 pounds, spend much of their time submerged in water, where they ambush crocodilians, large mammals, and other prey.

Green mamba

Snakes have very dry—not slimy—skin, which they shed periodically as their bodies grow and their scales become worn. Green mambas often snag their skin in the fork of a tree to expedite shedding.

August 1997, CNN reported that five Peruvian witnesses saw a "black boa constrictor the size of two passenger buses" slither through the jungle near their village. This extraordinary boa (whose typical length would range from 6 to 18½ feet, or about 1.8 to 5.6 m) was said to be a 130-footer (40 m), "felling trees and forging a ditch wide enough to drive a tractor through."

The record for the world's longest venomous serpent is held by an 18-foot 4-inch (5.49 m) king cobra captured in Thailand. In the United States, the record for a native (nonvenomous) snake found in the wild apparently belongs to a 9-foot 2-inch (3.02 m) gopher snake, followed by an 8-foot 7½-inch (2.63 m) Eastern indigo snake. There may well be a longer skin mounted on the wall of a saloon or roadside snake show somewhere, but the span of such a hide would not necessarily be a reliable indicator of the snake's true size, since treated skins can be stretched to anywhere from 25 to 50 percent of their original length.

Skin

"In this slimy Animal," a seventeenth-century philosopher declared on the subject of serpents, "are very many rare and excellent Observables." He was, it turns out, both wrong *and* right.

That snakes are "slimy" animals is one of those enduring myths that may never be put to rest. Snakes can be warm or cold (depending on the temperature of the substrate or the air); they can be wet (if recently snatched from a pond or stream); they can secrete fluids or feces—often quite rank-smelling—if excited or harassed; and, after shedding, they may feel slightly tacky, picking up particles of dirt or leaf litter. But slimy they are not. Eels, fish, slugs, mucus-secreting amphibians—these animals can feel "slimy"; snakes, on the other hand, have dry skin.

Their skin *is* rare and excellent, however, and certainly observable. A serpent's skin has three layers: a rough outer layer, made up of scales and plates; a thin middle layer of dividing cells; and a thick inner layer containing pigment cells. To most observers, the skin of a snake looks like a series of overlapping scales (rather like roofing shingles) or rows lined up side by side. In some species, the scales are smooth (e.g., the smooth green snake), while in others (the rough green snake, rattlesnakes, vipers), the scales are keeled, with a ridge running down the center.

These scales cannot be lifted or scraped off individually and "are not separate, removable parts, as they are in most fishes," Klauber explains; rather, they are created by folds or creases in the skin. Closer examination reveals skin between the scales—called interstitial skin—which becomes visible when a snake consumes a large meal or puffs up to startle a predator. Not all scales on a snake are the same size. The ventral (abdominal) scales, for example, are longer and arranged "like a tread on a bulldozer," herpetologists Carl Ernst and George Zug explain.

Chief among the functions of the skin are protection against physical injury and prevention against excessive moisture loss (desiccation). The skin also blocks ultraviolet rays, which, according to Leonard Appleby, "can be harmful if over-absorbed." Since the skin serves as the snake's outer barrier, it must be tough enough to resist constant wear from friction against other surfaces.

The skin of a snake is dry, not slimy, as commonly believed.

Brightly colored skin is typically a warning color for a venomous snake.

Eventually the scales become worn, however, and because they are already dead and thus cannot expand, the snake must periodically shed its outer skin. This process, known as ecdysis, can take up to two weeks, during which time the snake usually retreats, its eyes turn milky white, and the skin pigments become dull. If handled during this period, a snake may be unusually testy—probably because of its impaired vision.

To free itself of its old skin, a snake rubs its nose against a rough surface, sometimes yawning if necessary to stretch the skin; then, expanding and contracting its muscles, the snake gradually works its way out of the skin, leaving the translucent sheath inside out, like a sock that has just been peeled off. While a frog or salamander usually eats its cast-off skin, a snake will simply abandon its outer layer, with the imprint of every scale clearly discernible and the eye spectacle glistening.

Some species, like the heavy-bodied anaconda of South America, can shed their skin underwater, and arboreal snakes such as the green mamba may snag their skin in the fork of a tree to expedite shedding, leaving the skin draped from one tree to another.

Although an adult snake generally sheds about three or four times a year, the frequency can vary a good deal, depending on the animal's age, health, skin condition and hormones, external temperature and humidity, and other factors. Appleby, after studying the subject for more than forty years, has concluded that the most significant variable is the amount of food consumed. "A snake that feeds greedily," he says, "sheds its skin more often than does an indifferent feeder."

Many hikers who find a cast-off skin boast about the size of its former owner, but the length of the shed skin—which points in the opposite direction from the departed snake and permits precise species identification—is not a reliable measure, since the sloughed skin has covered the interstitial skin that "underlaps" the individual scales.

Color and Pattern

W. H. Hudson, the nineteenth-century author of *Green Mansions*, is considered an English writer, but he was born and lived for many years in South America, where he fell under the sway of serpents. Throughout his work, references to snakes and their beguiling colors and patterns appear with great frequency.

For Hudson, the scales of the fer-de-lance sparkle "like wind-crinkled water in the sun," the coral snake is a "brilliant deadly harlequin," and tree snakes are "threads of brilliant colour woven into the ever-changing varicoloured embroidery of Nature's mantle, seen vividly for an instant, then fading from sight."

The same colors and patterns that so entranced Hudson have likewise seduced many reluctant visitors to zoo reptile houses, where a spectrum of vivid colors from around the world is on display. There are the crimson reds of the pipe snake, mountain kingsnake, milk snake, and Halloween snake; the reddish pink of the coachwhip; the orange and red of the corn snake; the orange and black of the calico snake; the lavender of Costa Rica's banded tree snake; the pale blue of the yellow-lipped sea krait; the lemon yellow of the eyelash viper; and the emerald green of the boomslang, green mamba, and candy-striped South American vine snake.

Not all snakes, of course, sport brilliant

hues—and that is surely the secret of their success. Just as the bright warning colors of certain venomous species and their mimics enhance their odds for survival, so too can the dull browns and blacks and cryptic patterns of other snakes provide protective camouflage in their native habitats.

These colors are produced, for the most part, by pigments (chromatophores) present in skin cells. Sometimes, however, the effect of light on certain species' scales can cause two interesting phenomena: iridescence (a rainbowlike display) and "scattering" (radiance of the color blue). Although snakes are far less likely to "change" their colors than certain amphibians and other reptiles (such as the true chameleons), some do display seasonal color variations (death adders and Australian blacksnakes, for example), and a few, such as the Western rattlesnake, can darken or lighten their color quite quickly. Several boas, including Round Island and Madagascan tree boas, evidence slight color transformations from day to night, as do the Australian brownsnake, taipan, and Oenpelli python. Temperature, light, and other external stimuli can also induce color change, explains H. Bernard Bechtel, as can the daily rhythm of a snake's activities, including interaction with other individuals.

Among some species, such as milk snakes, newborns are often brighter than adults; as they age, their colors grow duller. Baby copperheads and cottonmouths may sport vivid yellow tails at birth, which they wriggle like caterpillars to attract prey. Juvenile emerald tree boas and green tree pythons aren't green at all during the first months or years of their lives (some are yellow, red, or even purple), and juvenile black racers aren't black—they're patterned

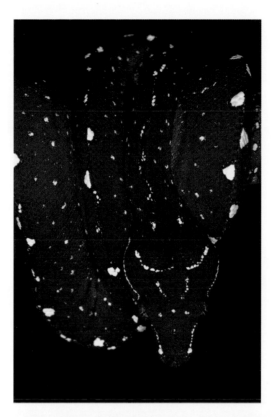

Juvenile green tree python
Left: *Offspring of green tree pythons from Australia and New Guinea, like those of emerald tree boas from South America, are nearly always brick red or bright yellow and do not acquire the rich green coloration of adults until six months of age or later. When resting on a tree limb, both species drape their coils evenly and position their head in the center.*

Eastern coral snake
Below: *The bright warning colors of the venomous Eastern coral snake are mimicked by various nonvenomous snakes. In some—but not all—species of coral snakes, red bands are bordered by yellow bands; among nonvenomous mimics, red and yellow do not touch.*

Burmese python
Above: *A Burmese python's cryptic coloration, which features dark brown, tan, and black blotches, offers excellent camouflage in Southeast Asian forests, foothills, marshes, and river valleys, where these large snakes lie motionless and ambush their prey.*

Albino Burmese python
Left: *Albino snakes such as this Burmese python lack melanins, yet their skin is seldom all white. Albino and leucistic specimens (the latter have normal-colored eyes) are especially popular with breeders and hobbyists.*

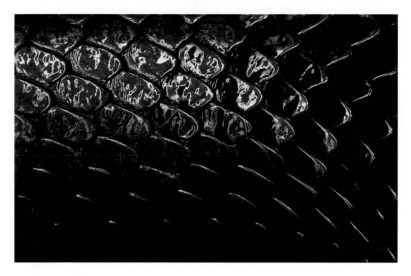

Eastern indigo snake
The scales of the Eastern indigo snake are shiny black with a beautiful dark-blue iridescence. The skin of this specimen is beginning to separate from the scales prior to shedding.

Green tree python
Close examination of the skin of an adult green tree python reveals a scattering of blue and yellow markings among the principally leaf-green scales. The "disruptive coloration" of these spots makes the python hard to detect among rain forest foliage dappled with sunlight.

Honduran milk snake
The distinct tricolored patterns of nonvenomous milk snakes from North, Central, and South America, including this Honduran milk snake, confuse many humans and predators, who associate the bright rings with those of dangerously venomous coral snakes.

"They are more ancient than the mammoth, and infinitely more beautiful. They are dry, cool and strong. The fitting and variation of the plates, the lovely colouring, the movement, their few thoughts: one could meditate upon them like a jeweler for months."
—T. H. White,
England Have My Bones, 1936

with gray, tan, or reddish brown blotches. Although rare in snakes, color differences between males and females are sometimes apparent.

Cryptic colors or disruptive patterns offer obvious benefits to snakes concealed against similar backgrounds, and stripes offer advantages to fast-moving species. The lateral stripes on garter and ribbon snakes, for example, make it "harder for a predator's eye to register the form of the snake," according to Scott Weidensaul, especially when the snake is darting through vegetation.

It is the banded species, however, not the striped ones, that have generated perhaps the liveliest herpetological debates. The bright warning (or "aposematic") colors of certain venomous snakes—most notoriously the coral snakes of North, Central, and South America—are often said to be "mimicked" by unrelated nonvenomous species.

"Since dangerous or distasteful animals are normally avoided by potential predators," J. L. Cloudsley-Thompson explains, "it is not surprising that many harmless species should, as a result of natural selection, have come to resemble them." This phenomenon, first formally described in the nineteenth century by naturalist Henry W. Bates, is known today as Batesian mimicry.

According to the Batesian hypothesis, harmless species such as milk snakes are confused with similarly (though not identically) banded coral snakes, since both sport alternating rings of red (or orange), yellow (or white), and black (or brown or gray). Skeptics, however, point out that coral snakes are primarily nocturnal (what good are colors at night?) and that brightly banded mimics such as milk

snakes and kingsnakes are not necessarily found near populations of coral snakes. How, these scientists wonder, can Batesian mimicry be applicable when the original prototypes aren't present or, when ranges do overlap, their habits make them inconspicuous—even to predators equipped with color vision? To this, Harry Greene responds that many New World coral snakes *are* active by day, and he and Roy McDiarmid add that the color red appears gray at night and thus performs a cryptic function as well. Studies have demonstrated that many birds have an aversion to snakes with red, yellow, and black bands, suggesting that the showy patterns of coral and milk snakes probably offer an evolutionary advantage for survival.

A companion hypothesis advanced by Fritz Muller, known today as Mullerian mimicry, posits that when two poisonous or unpalatable species resemble each other, they reinforce each other's protection by reducing overall predation. Some animals even mimic the patterns of very different species. For example, one species of dragonfly mimics small cobras, and the larvae of some South American butterflies and moths resemble vine snakes and vipers.

While the most beautifully colored snakes are usually the focus of human attention, their albino counterparts now exercise considerable appeal among breeders and hobbyists. "True" albinos—that is, those in which all melanins are absent, even in their eyes—are popular pets, as are leucistic varieties, which look like albinos but retain melanin in the eyes. Unlike most mammals and birds, albino snakes are seldom all white, according to Bechtel, and pale stripes or blotches are visible to some degree, generally in light shades of yellow, orange, or red.

*T*he tiger rattlesnake has stripes like the carnivorous cat for which it is named.

In Japan, an unusually large number of albino rat snakes have been discovered outside the city of Iwakuni and are believed to be the only naturally occurring population of albino snakes in the world. To protect this colony, the Japanese government has designated the snakes a "national monument."

Locomotion

"That rivulet of smooth silver—how does it flow?" John Ruskin pondered in a nineteenth-century essay on natural history. "It literally rows on the earth, with every scale for an oar; it bites the dust with the ridges of its body. Watch it when it moves slowly; a wave, but, without wind! a current, but with no fall! . . . Startle it: the winding stream will become a twisted arrow; the wave of poisoned life will lash through the grass like a cast lance."

Ruskin was attempting, with some difficulty, to describe the movements of a European adder. He wasn't the only one to find this task challenging: herpetologists, too, have found that describing snake locomotion isn't easy.

Snakes have at least four principal methods of movement. The most common, called lateral undulation, involves throwing the body into a series of loops or body waves and crawling horizontally, lashing the body from side to side. The body "literally swims along in a series of curves," says Carr, gaining traction by exerting pressure against grass, stones, and other irregularities in the ground.

The second type of movement is called rectilinear locomotion, or the "caterpillar crawl." Used by stocky snakes with heavy bodies, such as pythons, boas, and vipers, this method involves lifting the broad, flat belly scales and heaving them straight ahead in waves of muscular contractions, anchoring them as the snake pulls itself forward. This movement can be "so slow that it is barely perceptible," Richard Shine declares, "and may be very useful in creeping up to a prey item over a short space of open ground." The belly scales grip the ground like tractor treads, Carr explains, and leave behind a track like that of a dragged rope.

The third type of locomotion is the concertina movement, named for a musical instrument in the accordion family. Anchoring the rear part of the body, the snake stretches its head and neck forward and pushes from the rear (sometimes against the walls of a tunnel or channel), gripping the ground with the neck and pulling up the rest of the body. The concertina movement also enables snakes to climb trees. First, the snake draws its body up "like a spring" into a series of pleats, which it drapes over projections or irregularities in the bark, explains D. P. Maitland. To ascend, these body folds "push the snake's head forward until a new purchase point is found against which the snake can brace itself." The snake descends using the same technique.

The fourth method, sidewinding, is commonly used by snakes that dwell in deserts, where traction is difficult on loose sand. A sidewinder first throws a loop of the front end of its body forward for anchorage, then twists the rest of its body in a sideways undulation; before the tail reaches the ground, the head has already moved on to a new position.

"The best way to visualize the looping movement of a sidewinder," says Carr, "is to imagine a piece of wire coiled into slightly less than two loops and then rolled along the sand—it will make a series of

Mambas may be the fastest of all snakes, with an estimated top speed of 20 miles per hour (32 kph).

35

Eyelash viper
Above: *The venomous eyelash viper climbs trees and shrubs with ease. Though lacking limbs, snakes are able to climb by drawing up their body into a series of pleats and stretching the head and neck forward, securing a hold on irregularities in tree bark with their ventral scales.*

Water snake
Left: *North America's nonvenomous water snakes are excellent swimmers and divers. Some water snakes create a loop with their body to herd tadpoles and small fish into shallow water, where the small prey can be caught more easily.*

unconnected oblique tracks. . . . It touches the ground at only two points and unrolls its body along the dotted track until its head is extended enough to touch down for the beginning of another loop."

Although snakes rely primarily on these four methods, they use others from time to time. On a slick surface, for example, a snake may employ a movement called slide-pushing, or, in a threatening situation, it may even skid in a straight trajectory. "The appearance is of a snake flailing about on a smooth surface," note F. Harvey Pough et al., "but gradual forward progress is made." Some snakes "fling their heads forward, downward, or backward" when striking, Greene observes, while keeping the rear of their body coiled and anchored to the ground. Another method of locomotion, called saltation, involves throwing the entire body into the air; African horned adders use this movement when striking or attempting to escape. Other species reportedly "jump" at their prey, including the jumping viper of Central America, the Asian saw-scaled viper, and the Pacific viper boa.

There is also the aerial locomotion of the so-called flying snakes, which appear to glide through the air from high in the rain forest canopy. These snakes, from southern Asia, flatten their bodies and launch themselves in controlled falls to escape enemies or reach the ground.

In 1916, after a hunter presented a Borneo museum with a live snake he claimed had "flown" out of a tree, the skeptical museum curator promptly carried the snake upstairs to the veranda and tossed it into the air. "I was disappointed to see it fall in writhing coils to the ground, which it hit with a thud," curator Robert Shelford

wrote. "Then I allowed the snake merely to . . . glide rapidly through my hands. . . . There can be no doubt that the hinged ventral scales of these snakes, enabling them to draw the belly inwards, are a modification of structure rendering a parachute flight possible."

Many snakes also swim on occasion, undulating their body from side to side. Water snakes and cottonmouths spend a great deal of time in freshwater or on branches overhanging water and even turn up in brackish water or swim in salt water between islands. Other species may enter water to escape predators or to hunt for frogs and fish.

The sea snakes and sea kraits of the Indo-Pacific region move only with great difficulty on land, where they "squirm and flounder about in a pitiable way," says Carr, due to the absence of broad belly scales. Except for one freshwater species, these snakes live in salt water, where the paddlelike tails on their rubbery, compressed bodies effectively push against the water.

Whatever their method of locomotion, snakes generally impress observers as being quite swift—and, for short distances, many are. Timing a snake requires considerable patience and luck, however, since snakes rarely traverse level ground in a straight line, as humans with stopwatches would prefer. Nonetheless, the black mamba is believed to be the world's "fastest" snake, and John Nichol claims a mamba was once timed at 8 miles (13 km) an hour for a short distance. Other speedy serpents include North America's black racer, clocked at about 3.7 miles (5.96 km) per hour, and coachwhip, at 3.6 miles (5.8 km) per hour.

Mangrove snakes may spend their entire lives in trees; coiled on tree limbs and hanging over rivers and streams, they hunt at night for birds, bats, rodents, frogs, lizards, and snakes.

Vision

Snakes, it is often said, project a sense of mystery, and to many observers the serpent's "unwinking" eye is an enigma. Confronted in the wild by an unblinking serpent, early American explorers were convinced these creatures could stare down or "hypnotize" birds or other prey (they can't); some even insisted snakes could hypnotize humans.

It is true that snakes do not wink or blink, but that is because they do not have movable eyelids. Their eyes are protected by a spectacle, or brille—a large, transparent scale that shields the eyeball and is shed with each molt. (Spectacles are really modified lids that have fused together and become transparent.)

"We still know relatively little about vision in snakes," admits Shine, but evolutionary biologists suspect that modern snakes evolved from ancestors—presumably lizards—that had no need for lids because they lived underground or were nocturnal. (Recent fossil evidence of a primitive snake that had vestiges of hind legs and probably lived in the sea may suggest a lidless aquatic ancestor.)

Comparative anatomist Gordon Walls, after studying the eyes of animals for many years, concluded that "snakes alone have wrung as many changes upon their visual-cell patterns as have all the other vertebrates put together." Snakes' eyes degenerated after a lengthy underground existence shunning the sunlight, Walls deduced, but once these creatures returned to the surface, "the losses and defects were so numerous that the snakes had almost to invent the vertebrate eye all over again."

"Nothing like this tremendous feat has occurred in any other vertebrate group, so far as we can tell," Walls marveled. "If any-thing could make a snake-hater learn respect and admiration for this abused group of animals, it would be the study of their eyes. The writer speaks from personal experience."

One of the more fascinating aspects of a serpent's eye is its method of focusing. Unlike all other reptiles, birds, and mammals, snakes are able to move the rounded lens in their eye forward and backward relative to the retina—like the movable focusing lens of a camera, with the retina in the role of the film. Another unusual aspect is the presence of color in the snake's lens, which Walls discovered when he accidentally ruptured the eye of a Montpellier snake from southwestern Europe. Walls recognized that a yellow lens, like yellow glass, would increase visual acuity and sharpen vision by absorbing refracted violet rays and filtering out blue light. He then correctly predicted that the swiftest serpents, such as racers, would have the yellowest lenses, permitting them to see and chase fast-moving prey.

The pupils of snakes are interesting, too—generally round and moderate-sized in diurnal (day-active) species, closing tightly in very bright sunlight, and usually large and vertical in nocturnal species and able to open wider. The pronounced curvature of the cornea (eyeball) in boomslangs and whipsnakes, whose eyes are set relatively high on the side of the head, permits an enhanced field of vision and greater depth perception; such an adaptation is particularly advantageous to arboreal and terrestrial snakes that feed on fast-moving lizards.

Not all snakes, however, have a round or vertical pupil. Some vine snakes and twig snakes have horizontal keyhole-shaped pupils, which extend their binocular vision

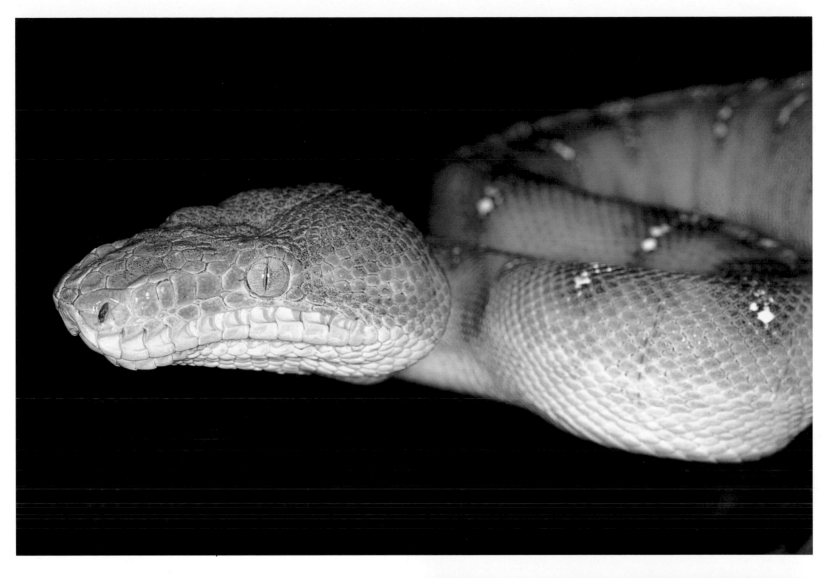

Emerald tree boa

Above: *Most snakes that hunt at night, including this adult emerald tree boa, have vertical pupils. These vertical slits open in low-light conditions to allow more light to enter the eye.*

Western ribbon snake

Right: *Large round pupils are usually associated with diurnal (day-active) hunters, such as ribbon snakes, garter snakes, and whipsnakes. Although snake eyes lack traditional eyelids, a transparent spectacle protects the eye.*

(the area seen by both eyes at the same time) to about 45°—well beyond the 30° typical of most snakes. The vine snake's vision is further enhanced by a depression running along each side of its snout, which "more or less gets the elongated pointed snout out of the snake's line of sight," Peter Brazaitis and Myrna Watanabe report.

Whether or not some species are capable of color vision is currently unresolved. Snake eyes apparently lack oil droplets, which in other vertebrates, Shine points out, are used for color vision. This might explain why color differences between the sexes are so rare in snakes, he says, since subtle or even prominent variations would go unnoticed.

Curiously, Australian Ken Zimmerman has discovered a light-sensitive organ, or photoreceptor, on the tail of the olive sea snake. This "eyelike" sense organ "sounds impossible," Shine marvels, but studies suggest these snakes use their tails to help them hide from predators in crevices during the daytime.

Smell and Taste

"A snake travels by its tongue as a dog travels by its nose," biologist Ann Morgan writes, but dogs, frogs, and humans have tongues, too—they just use them for different purposes. The "invisible highways" traveled by snakes provide them with information that would make most humans envious.

A snake's forked tongue is perhaps its most celebrated organ. Aristotle thought it permitted "a twofold pleasure from savours," doubling the sensation of taste. Other early scientists believed the bifurcated (two-branched) tongue was for "picking the Dirt out of their Noses," stinging enemies or prey, warning intruders, catch-ing insects, hearing, touching, or conveying intelligence.

The tines, or pointed tips, at the end of a snake's tongue intrigued observers because the snake clearly used them for some sensory function—why else would it flick its tongue out so frequently when confronting a new environment? Surely it had something to do with taste or smell, scientists reasoned, even though the snake already had a functional pair of nostrils.

In fact, the tongue did prove to be an organ for chemoreception, but its role is essentially that of a delivery mechanism. Flicking the tongue to the front or side (or even over the head), the snake samples scent particles in the air and on the ground and delivers them inside the mouth to the Jacobson's, or vomeronasal, organs.

Like paired eyes or ears, explains herpetologist Kurt Schwenk, the forked tongue provides "a kind of 'stereo smell'" that permits snakes to "assess whether there was a

Mangrove snake
Facing page: *A snake's forked tongue picks up scent particles and delivers them to a tissue pad in the mouth that is pressed against the roof of the mouth. The sensory cells of the Jacobson's organ then analyze these particles, enabling the snake to distinguish prey, predators, and prospective mates.*

Copperhead
Below: *A snake's nostrils are primarily respiratory openings, while the pits on the forward head of a copperhead and other pit vipers are for sensing heat. The flicking tongue is a chemoreceptive device that gathers scent particles in the air and on the ground.*

Albino Western diamondback rattlesnake

Left: *A pair of deep cavities, or pits, located between the nostrils and eyes of a Western diamondback rattlesnake and other pit vipers detect infrared heat and are sensitive to minute changes in temperature.*

Juvenile emerald tree boa

Below: *Heat-sensitive pits on the lips of many boas and pythons enable these snakes to pinpoint with great accuracy the location of endothermic (warm-blooded) prey. According to herpetologist Richard Shine, many snakes have "small sensory pits on the scales around their snout," the function of which is not fully understood.*

difference in the strength of that chemical on the left side versus the right side."

The tips transfer molecules or chemical cues to a tissue pad on the floor of the mouth, Ernst and Zug explain, rather than inserting them directly into the vomeronasal organs, as was formerly believed; the pad "is then pressed against the roof of the mouth, transferring odor particles to the Jacobson's organs." Receptor cells send impulses to the olfactory lobes in the brain, which analyze the chemical cues. The snake's paired nostrils also contribute to this "smelling" process by inhaling odors, but snakes breathe "much less frequently than mammals," Klauber points out, and their nostrils are primarily respiratory openings.

A snake's tongue seems unusual not only because of its role in chemoreception and olfaction, but also because it isn't used for drinking water or tasting. Snakes do drink, of course, but they submerge their snouts into water and pump with their throats. Taste buds, insofar as they have been identified at all, appear not on the tongue but on the roof of the mouth in tissue beside the teeth.

Heat-Sensitive Pits

When explorers first encountered rattlesnakes in the Americas, many were puzzled by the strange "pits" visible on each side of the rattler's snout between the nostril and the eye. Did these remarkable snakes have extra nostrils, some wondered, or, lacking eyelids, did rattlers have special tear ducts, glands, or ears?

In the 1930s, G. K. Noble and Arthur Schmidt published the results of a series of experiments that resolved the mystery: the pits, they said, were short-range thermoreceptive devices that respond to the presence of heat. (More recently, Greene has observed that the pits are "probably infrared imaging devices," not simply thermal receptors.)

Previously, scientists knew that lighted matches and electric lightbulbs excited rattlesnakes, but when lightbulbs were covered with black material to eliminate light as a possible stimulus, rattlesnakes *still* grew excited and would strike at the source. When Noble and Schmidt systematically blocked off their snakes' sense organs, they discovered that rattlers still struck at the lightbulbs with amazing accuracy—suggesting that radiant heat, rather than light, triggered the reactions.

Closer examination eventually revealed that each pit has two chambers, separated by a thin membrane equipped with nerve endings. The nerves in this membrane are extraordinarily sensitive to the slightest change in temperature—in some species as little as 0.002° F (0.001° C).

"Thus the facial pit is a genuine 'sixth sense,'" herpetologists Karl Schmidt and Robert Inger conclude, "a peculiarly effective aid to the snakes that kill warm-blooded prey by means of venom injected during a sudden strike, and the more essential because the snakes hunt primarily at night."

Pit vipers, including copperheads, cottonmouths, rattlesnakes, and some Latin American vipers, aren't the only snakes with facial pits. Many pythons and boas (though not boa constrictors or several others) also have pits, which are located along the lips. In these serpents, as many as thirteen pairs of shallow pits (or "labial dimples") line the upper lip and sometimes the lower lip, suggesting to leery observers that the snake is curling its lips like a snarling dog.

Green tree pythons have heat-sensitive pits on each side of their heads that can detect the presence of birds and other animals at a distance of up to 1 foot 6 inches (45.7 cm).

Macmahon's viper

Below, top: *Macmahon's viper, an inhabitant of desert regions of Iran, Pakistan, and Afghanistan, uses a shuffling movement to bury itself in the sand, where it protects itself from extreme heat and lies in wait to ambush small rodents and lizards.*

Western diamondback rattlesnake in Sonoran Desert

Below, bottom: *Rattlesnakes and other species bask in sunlight or on sun-warmed ground during certain seasons (early spring and late fall, for example), at higher elevations, and during brief periods of the day to regulate their body temperature. Too much direct heat, however, can kill a rattlesnake.*

Like the loreal pits of rattlers, these labial pits help pythons and boas to detect temperature differences between endothermic (warm-blooded) prey and the background environment and to locate the prey's position with extraordinary precision, even in the dark. Some members of this family that lack pits along their lips are equipped with heat-sensitive receptors beneath the scales on their snouts, and a few vipers without pits, such as the Russell's viper and puff adder, are apparently sensitive to some thermal stimulation.

Thermoregulation

People commonly believe that warm-blooded animals (endotherms) such as birds and mammals are superior to the so-called cold-blooded animals (ectotherms), including reptiles and amphibians and nearly all other animals, because they have an internal energy source and are therefore subject to less variation in body temperature. But snakes aren't cold-blooded at all (their preferred body temperature is around 86° F/30° C), and scientists now recognize certain advantages to ectothermy.

In addition to eating less frequently, snakes can survive on much less food than birds or mammals of the same approximate weight because they do not need as much fuel. According to Shine, a mammal requires "at least ten times the amount of food . . . to keep itself alive as would a reptile of the same body size, [and] under some circumstances . . . up to a hundred times more."

On the other hand, ectotherms cannot maintain intense metabolic activity for extended periods of time; bursts of speed or other strenuous physical activity quickly deplete the oxygen in their muscles, leaving snakes "exhausted often after only a few minutes," Shine reports. Young snakes tire especially quickly and are even slower to recuperate.

While snakes are sometimes derided because they appear to be at the mercy of their environment, this is hardly the case. In many ways, snakes are the masters of their environment—whether subterranean, terrestrial, arboreal, or aquatic—because they are able to regulate their body temperatures by taking advantage of external sources of heat, from the ground, air, water, direct or reflected solar rays, or each other.

To maintain a preferred body temperature without overchilling or overheating, snakes simply shift their position, withdrawing or extending portions of their bodies into areas where heat can be absorbed. As a result, snakes shuttle back and forth a good deal from sunshine to shade. Snakes raise their body temperature by basking, one of their favored and most visible activities, which accounts for their unfortunate preference for sun-warmed asphalt. Blacktop pavement retains heat well into the night, thus attracting nocturnal species, and, as it absorbs the sun's rays in the morning, it provides warmth for diurnal species that have just emerged. Either way, roads spell trouble for snakes, and highway mortality rates are exceptionally high. Because of their body length, snakes are easy targets for fast-moving vehicles—and, to make matters worse, some drivers deliberately swerve to kill a snake when they notice one on or beside a road.

While highways are a welcome, if dangerous, source of warmth, too much direct heat can result in death. Since snakes lack sweat glands and cannot perspire, they will die if unable to escape from dangerously hot conditions. At temperatures around 113° F (45° C), "irreversible muscular heat-rigor ensues" that can kill a rattlesnake in ten to twelve minutes, Klauber reports.

Conversely, a quick drop in temperature, or extended involuntary exposure to low temperatures, will cause what Klauber calls "benumbing lethargy" or death by freezing. However, snakes that undergo cold narcosis, or stupor, can be revived under certain circumstances. I recall a fellow nature counselor whose pet boa constrictor "died" after exposure to unexpectedly low night-time temperatures in northern Wisconsin. While mourning the loss of his beloved boa the next morning, he set her glass cage out in the sun, and—miraculously—she thawed out and was restored to her former self in just a few hours.

One obvious strategy for absorbing heat is to capitalize on body color, since a species' light or dark coloration helps to regulate its temperature during daytime or nighttime activity. Generally, dark pigmentation expedites absorption of available heat, while lighter pigmentation reflects

available heat.

Other strategies of thermoregulation include coiling up the body to reduce exposed surface areas, or, in cases where female pythons remain with their eggs, "shivering" (that is, generating heat by contracting muscles in regular, spasmodic motions). Prior to hibernation, many species aggregate in the vicinity of communal dens, where they may coil up together during overwintering. Such massing together of large numbers of snakes, especially in northern climates, may be explained by a shortage of available underground chambers where snakes can avoid freezing.

Venom

When Douglas Adams, author of *The Hitchhiker's Guide to the Galaxy*, was preparing for a field expedition to view some of the world's endangered animals, he began to worry he might encounter dangerous

Timber rattlesnake

Snake venom is a highly specialized saliva that immobilizes prey and begins the digestive process from the inside out even before the prey is swallowed. Timber rattlesnakes and other venomous species often pull back after striking their prey, trailing the scent of an envenomated victim and waiting for it to die.

"Wear baggy trousers. When a snake strikes, it starts to inject venom as soon as it hits something. If you've got baggy trousers, most of the venom will just get squirted down the inside of your trousers, which is better than it being squirted down the inside of your leg."
—Dr. Struan Sutherland, expert on snake venoms, quoted in Douglas Adams and Mark Carwardin, *Last Chance To See*, 1990

45

snakes. For reassurance and advice, he sought out Australian venom authority Struan Sutherland.

"Can't stand all these poisonous creatures, all these snakes and insects and fish and things," Sutherland told Adams. "Stupid things, biting everybody. And then people expect me to tell them what to do about it. I'll tell them what to do. Don't get bitten in the first place. That's the answer."

"So what do we do if we get bitten by something deadly, then?" Adams pressed.

"Well, what do you think you do?" Sutherland barked. "You die, of course. That's what deadly means."

Fortunately, not everyone bitten by a venomous snake dies, and so many different factors are involved in the circumstances of any given bite that it's difficult to estimate the odds of survival or death. That's partly because researchers know a lot more about snake venoms today than they did just a few decades ago.

It was once believed that snake venoms fell into one of two categories: hemotoxins and neurotoxins. Now, however, scientists recognize that every type of snake venom contains "elements of the other," says authority John Nichol, "and all of them consist of a cocktail made up from varying proportions" of at least eight types of ingredients, including neurotoxins, hemorrhagins, anticoagulants, antibacterial agents, ferments for digesting, and substances that destroy red and white blood cells and cause blood clots.

Although most people routinely refer to snakes as "poisonous" or "nonpoisonous," scientists prefer to use the term "venomous" to distinguish the true method of envenomation. A poison, explains toxicologist Findlay Russell, is "a substance that, in relatively small amounts, produces death or impairs seriously the functions of organs or tissues. Poisonous animals are generally regarded to be those creatures whose tissues . . . are toxic"—toads, frogs, newts, and pufferfish, for example. "Poisoning by these forms usually takes place through ingestion of their flesh," while venom is delivered "during the act of biting or stinging." Thus, Russell concludes, "all venomous animals are poisonous, but not all poisonous animals can be considered venomous."

While moviegoers routinely expect the very worst from any serpent that slithers across the silver screen, only about 375 of the approximately 2,700 recognized species of snakes are considered venomous, according to Russell, and the odds of being bitten by a venomous snake are even less than those of being struck by lightning. ("More people are killed and injured annually in their bathtubs in this country than by snakebite," Klauber writes, "but it must be admitted that a good many more people encounter bathtubs than snakes.")

In the United States, snakes with venom include cottonmouths and copperheads, two species of coral snakes, sixteen species of rattlesnakes (including massasaugas and pigmy rattlers), and the occasional yellow-bellied sea snake that washes ashore on the California coastline. But there are also a number of rear-fanged snakes in the United States with enlarged teeth at the back of their mouth. Venomous though not necessarily dangerous, these commonly overlooked snakes include the brown vine, lyre, black-striped, hooknose, Northern cat-eyed, night, crowned, flathead, blackhead, and blackhood snakes, as well as others that trigger allergic reactions among humans.

The venom of the Western diamondback rattlesnake attacks blood cells, causing rapid hemorrhaging from breakdown of vascular tissues.

Coral cobra
Facing page: *The coral cobra is a short burrowing species from southern Africa that exhales air explosively when harassed. Although these snakes often feign death when threatened, experts warn that their venom is dangerously neurotoxic, attacking the nervous system and stopping the heart and lungs.*

King cobras boast enormous venom glands and can inject a staggering amount of venom.

Venomous snakes are the "aristocrats" of the snake world, Pope says, because "they alone can secure food and protect themselves without exerting great muscular effort." This points up the evolutionary utility of fangs and venom glands: once a snake strikes its prey and injects venom, it doesn't have to engage in a potentially harmful struggle with its food; instead, it can just wait for it to succumb. The bite of a venomous snake can kill a small animal in seconds or minutes and can destroy tissues and organs in humans or cause death.

Estimates suggest about 300,000 people worldwide are victims of venomous snakebites each year, and, according to Russell, close to 100,000 of these snakebites are fatal. Although an extraordinary array of variables comes into play when a human is bitten—including the age, size, gender, and health of the victim and the snake; the site, nature, and number of bites; the species of snake; the condition of the fangs; and the amount of venom injected—a few generalizations can be made regarding "deadliness" of certain species. The inland taipan of Australia is cited by Shine as the "deadliest snake in the world," due to its potent venom, long fangs, and penchant for multiple bites; by these criteria, the sea snakes, eastern brownsnake, king cobra, and black mamba are all close runners-up. If, on the other hand, volume of venom injected per bite is the primary consideration, then the Gaboon viper, Eastern diamondback rattlesnake, and bushmaster are usually cited as the most dangerous venomous serpents.

The venom of species with chiefly hemotoxic properties (including copperheads, cottonmouths, and most North American rattlesnakes) attacks the victim's circulatory system, destroying the walls of blood vessels, causing seepage of blood underneath the skin, and breaking down tissues. Neurotoxins, on the other hand, attack the nervous system and kill by stopping the heart and lungs.

Traditional on-site first aid for snakebite victims once emphasized "cut and suck" procedures—cutting open the wound with a blade to permit blood to flow and sucking the envenomation site or squeezing a small rubber suction cup in an attempt to prevent venom from entering the bloodstream. Today, however, researchers recognize that such "treatment" can actually cause serious damage. (Cutting X-shaped slits across puncture wounds makes matters worse by traumatizing the victim and damaging skin and muscles, while sucking out the venom can introduce toxins into the bloodstream of the person applying first aid if they have bad teeth, mouth ulcers, or gum disease.)

"It was once thought that the venom was carried in the bloodstream, so painful and dangerous tourniquets were recommended to isolate the circulation in the bitten part of the body," Shine explains. "Fortunately, this *isn't* the way the venom reaches the general circulation. Most of it is in the lymph not the blood at this stage, and the lymphatic vessels run very close to the skin."

Probably the best advice for dealing with snakebite is to keep the patient calm, eliminate muscle movement, and wrap an elastic bandage around the elevated limb to slow down the lymphatic flow (a splint is highly recommended). The next course of action is to transport the victim as quickly as possible to a hospital—hence the declaration by some emergency medical personnel that the best first aid is "a set of car keys."

In the event of cardiac or respiratory arrest, standard cardiopulmonary resuscitation (CPR) is recommended; experts Jonathan Campbell and William Lamar also suggest establishing an intravenous line with isotonic fluids, if available, prior to transport. And no matter how many larger-than-life film heroes have belted down a quart of whiskey after being bitten by a rattlesnake, such a "remedy" would in fact act as a dangerous stimulant and induce alcohol poisoning if ingested in large quantities. In addition, it is vitally important to identify the species of snake or bring along its body, so that hospital personnel can administer the appropriate antivenom (also known as antivenin).

At the medical facility, the victim is tested for an allergic reaction to horse serum before being treated with the antivenom, which is made of antibodies and immunoglobulin proteins taken from the blood of horses injected with mild doses of venom solutions. Venom is supplied by experts who "milk" venomous snakes, holding a specimen with its fangs exposed over a membrane-covered container or glass dish. As the snake bites through the membrane (sometimes slight pressure is applied to the venom glands), venom is discharged into the container. The drops of venom are then placed in a centrifuge, which separates toxic enzymes from debris, and the liquid is later freeze-dried. If kept away from heat, light, and dampness, freeze-dried venom crystals can retain their potency for many years.

Recently, researchers and drug companies have conducted experiments with snake venoms to find alternatives to horses for the making of antivenoms, since allergic reactions, or serum sickness, occur in up to 75 percent of recipients. In studies at the University of Arizona and at the University of Wisconsin, sheep, goats, and chicken eggs have been substituted for horses, and the antibodies produced in these experiments may yield antivenoms that can be used effectively on humans. Therapeutic Antibodies, a Nashville-based biopharmaceuticals company that harvests antibodies from Australian and Welsh sheep injected with toxins, currently markets two venomous-snakebite antidotes in Europe and in West Africa and is in the final stages of testing an antivenom for rattlesnake bites.

Internal Organs and Functions

Snakes, a biologist once remarked, are "superlatively streamlined examples of an efficiency of omission." But the "omission" of arms and legs, not to mention other niceties such as feet, toes, wings, fins, claws, nails, hooves, and toe pads, makes the snake a marvel not just of external but also internal streamlining.

The skeletal system, for example, differs significantly from that of mammals. Whereas humans have only 32 vertebrae, snakes have from 180 to 435. Lacking a pectoral girdle (collarbone and shoulder blades) and, for the most part, a pelvic girdle (although some species retain vestiges of this girdle, called "spurs"), snakes have systematically evolved a stable system; the accessory spines, or ribs, are attached to the vertebral column and connected not to a breastbone (sternum) but, rather, to each other and to the skin by elastic muscles. This system offers amazing flexibility, allowing the snake to distend its body when consuming large prey. While the sheer length of the spinal column and delicate nature of the bone structure make snakes especially vulnerable, their skeletal

*S*nakes have from 180 to 435 vertebrae. While the sheer length of the spinal column and delicate nature of the bone structure make snakes especially vulnerable, their skeletal system is not only highly efficient but also virtually unique.

system is not only highly efficient but also virtually unique.

The skull is a remarkable structure, too, designed to accommodate the feeding needs of a vertebrate that lacks hands. Amazingly, the anatomy of the lower jaw permits a snake to engulf its prey whole. Because the two halves of the lower jaw can actually separate and move independently, and because the upper and lower jaws are not fused to one another or to the cranium (instead, they are held together by elastic ligaments), the gape of the snake can accommodate an object up to three times the diameter of the snake's head. To permit the snake to breathe when food blocks its mouth and throat, the opening of the windpipe—called the glottis—is periodically pushed out between the object and the floor of the mouth like a snorkel.

Although some species, such as worm snakes and blind snakes, sport only a few teeth, most have rows of sharp, recurved teeth, loosely attached to the inner ridges of the lower jaw and outer portion of the upper jaw, which hold the prey firmly in place. Some snakes, such as cobras, mambas, coral snakes, and sea snakes, are also equipped with short fangs at the front of the mouth, with which they inject venom while "chewing" their prey. Vipers and pit vipers, on the other hand, have long, curved fangs—not unlike hypodermic needles—that inject venom deeper into the prey; these fangs are hinged and fold back into the roof of the mouth when not in use.

Finally, the so-called rear-fanged snakes (e.g., vine, lyre, and cat-eyed snakes) have one or two supplementary pairs of enlarged teeth at the rear of the mouth; these teeth, which are grooved in many species, carry secretions from the Duvernoy's gland that paralyze the prey as the snake "chews"

> "Fillet of a fenny snake,
> In the cauldron boil and bake;
> Eye of newt, and toe of frog,
> Wool of bat, and tongue of dog,
> Adder's fork, and blindworm's sting,
> Lizard's leg, and howlet's wing—
> For a charm of pow'rful trouble
> Like a hell-broth boil and bubble."
> —William Shakespeare, "Macbeth"

Gaboon viper
Snakes often yawn after a meal. This Gaboon viper has just consumed a rat and is stretching its mouth to realign its jaws.

it. Since a snake's teeth and fangs are frequently broken or shed, replacement teeth develop from "buds" on the internal wall of the jaw and are kept in reserve behind the existing ones until needed.

The respiratory system is also modified to meet the needs of the snake. Perhaps due to limited room in its slender body, the snake's left lung is ordinarily very small or missing altogether, while the right lung is considerably extended. By expanding its rib cage, a snake sucks air into its lungs; when it relaxes its muscles, it pumps the air back out. Toward the tail, the hind portion of the right lung functions as an air sac, rather like a fish's swim bladder, pumping air through the vascularized lungs.

To ease the passage of a meal down its gullet (which John Crompton calls "a kind of waiting room for the chamber of horrors beyond"), the snake lubricates its prey with saliva. Digestion actually begins in the mouth, where the oral glands secrete various digestive enzymes or proteins. These glandular secretions may also help to cleanse the teeth.

Next encountered is the stomach, a muscular tube that expands to accommodate large meal items. The digestive process is fairly slow in snakes—the total time may be five or six days, on average—and the snake will be in no great hurry to find another meal anytime soon. Prey injected with venom is given a head start, breaking down even before it is ingested.

"Snakes can store great quantities of reserve material and thus be prepared for long fasts," Pope explains. "In this ability, they surpass all warm-blooded animals." Such fasts by snakes in captivity are relatively common: pythons and anacondas have been known to go more than a year between meals, and a rock python once

went two years and nine months.

Waste products that remain after digestion, including such things as hair, feathers, and claws, are excreted from the cloaca as feces or as a highly insoluble, pastelike substance known as uric acid, which is produced by the kidneys. (Snakes do not secrete liquid urine.) Pope calls the cloaca "literally a catchall. The anus is merely the exit from the cloaca to the exterior."

Anyone who has ever handled snakes has, at some point, discovered these animals discharge a variety of repugnant fluids from skin glands or the cloaca—an ingenious defense mechanism that causes many meddling humans or would-be predators to drop the snake after getting a whiff of the excretion. The ingredients of these foul-smelling discharges include not only by-products of digestion but also musk-gland secretions and sex-related pheromones. Among the more aromatic species are the cottonmouth, whose musk is likened to the aroma of a billy goat; the European ringed snake, said to smell like a mixture of garlic and mouse manure; the copperhead, reported to smell like a cucumber; the fox snake, which secretes a pasty substance with a foxlike odor; and angry rattlesnakes, which cowboys swear have the pungent aroma of a wet dog or green watermelon.

The snake's slender heart, like many of its other organs, is unusually elongated, and it can be located "if one strokes the snake's underside from the head downward in a massaging manner," says herpetologist Heini Hediger. "Snakes do not like to be grabbed on this part of the body, and they usually react defensively."

A snake's heart consists anatomically of three chambers—left and right atria and one ventricle—but, as F. Harvey Pough

Blood python
*The blood python of Southeast Asia and other snakes
that swallow large prey can go long periods of time
between feedings. In captivity, some pythons and anacondas have been known to go a year or longer between meals.*

et al. explain, "it is functionally five-chambered because contraction of the ventricle turns its single chamber into three chambers." It was once believed that oxygenated blood from the lungs mixed with deoxygenated blood entering the single ventricle, but recent experiments suggest that snake and lizard hearts are more functionally sophisticated than originally suspected.

The snake's brain, while said to be more complex than that of an amphibian, is at the same time less complex than the brain of other animals that require a nervous system to service their appendages. The snake's spinal cord of nervous tissue is quite long, running the length of the spinal column, and is particularly vulnerable to damage, especially from cars and trucks.

Near the vent at the base of the tail are the snake's reproductive organs—ovaries and oviducts in females; testes, sperm duct, and hemipenes in males. In a quirk of evolutionary development, every male snake is equipped with two copulatory organs, which are smooth in some species and covered with sharp spines or hooks in others. Only one hemipenis is used at a time during copulation, however, alternating with the other when the interval between matings is short, according to Richard Zweifel. The organs, which are kept in place by retractor muscles, are everted from the male's cloaca during mating.

Reproduction

"Among reptiles," Pope once wrote, "the snakes have been especially successful in hiding their sex life from the eyes of man." Indeed, relatively few humans encounter snakes in the act of coupling. But reports supplied by naturalists, zookeepers, and breeders, and data generated by scientists who track snakes with implanted radio transmitters, now offer humans a more intimate glimpse of the reproductive traits of these secretive creatures.

If a herpetologist were to write a *Kama Sutra* for snakes, its contents would surprise most humans. Exotic oils and "perfumes" (called pheromones) prepare the partners for arousal, followed by much sensual rubbing, tongue action, and even chasing. In some instances, male "combat dances" precede the courtship. Although the female usually remains passive, she sometimes drags the male off to a site more to her liking. Each male is equipped with not one but two copulatory organs, and sometimes the coupling will go on for twenty-four hours or longer. Multiple matings are common, and, at some sites, males flock to available females and form giant "balls" of writhing bodies.

Much of this may sound preposterous, but close examination of the serpent libido reveals some fascinating behavior. During snake courtship and mating, Shine ob-

Blanchard's milk snake
Egg-laying species such as milk snakes and kingsnakes generally deposit their eggs in rotting stumps and logs, under rocks, or in abandoned burrows. This neonate (newborn) Blanchard's milk snake emerged from its egg less than one hour before it was photographed.

Carolina pigmy rattlesnake "combat dance"

Above: *A pair of male Carolina pigmy rattlesnakes engage in a ritualized "combat dance," rearing up and attempting to force each other's head and neck to the ground. Eventually, after one snake is pinned, it ends the competition abruptly and crawls away.*

Carolina pigmy rattlesnakes

Right: *During courtship, a male Carolina pigmy rattlesnake moves jerkily over the body of a female, flicking his tongue and slowing rubbing his chin across her body.*

serves, the female "generally remains passive, while the male moves around in a jerky, excited fashion." Describing the courtship of two Northern copperheads, Henry Fitch refers to the "spasmodic jerks" of the male as he forces his posterior under the female "with a rippling movement" and then moves "convulsively," disengaging from his position and thrashing about wildly.

Chemoreception, rather than visual cues, is the key to snake amour. The male locates sexually active females by flicking his tongue and picking up a trail of pheromones (tiny pollenlike chemicals) and other odors left on the substrate by the female's skin glands or cloacal glands. Upon finding a female, the male may explore her body with his tongue and rub his chin along her neck and back (black racers, among others, may bite the female's neck).

Water snakes, garter snakes, and several other species have sensitive tubercles, or nodules, on their chins, which respond to this rubbing and stimulate the male. The sight of a throng of male garter or water snakes endeavoring to arouse a female can be quite astonishing, Pope says, especially when the eager snakes "all try to rub their chins at once."

Some, such as the Aesculapian snake of Europe, increase their speed during the arousal stage of courtship, "dashing wildly through field, over boulder, up onto bush and down again, like creatures gone mad," Pope notes. Males of some species wrap their body around the female or raise her off the ground to bring their vents together, and some pythons and boas scratch the female with tiny spurs—the evolutionary remnants of hind legs.

One of the more fascinating rituals performed by some serpents is the so-called combat dance. Because it is virtually impossible to distinguish between the sexes from a distance, persons fortunate enough to glimpse a combat dance are often baffled by all the writhing and pushing; some assume they are witnessing copulation, while others are convinced it is homosexual activity. Over the years, however, field researchers and zookeepers have come to recognize this as competition between rival males (generally pit vipers, true vipers, Australian elapids, and some pythons), during which the two snakes intertwine their bodies while each attempts to press the other down and force it off balance.

These bouts vary in length, Chris Mattison says, until "eventually one of the males, usually the smaller individual, concedes defeat and crawls away." The wrestling may be a test of male strength (biting is rarely involved), a form of social domination, or a claim to a particular female or territory.

It was once commonly believed that snakes in the wild mated only in the spring or early summer, but that assumption is no longer accepted. True, it appears that most males court females shortly after their emergence from hibernation, but some, such as pit vipers and adders, mate in late summer or fall. In these cases, females demonstrate a remarkable evolutionary trait: they store the male's sperm in special pockets in their oviducts until a more opportune time for fertilization. Generally, this fertilization occurs the following spring, but not always. In captivity, an indigo snake once laid eggs four years after insemination, a banded cat-eyed snake after six years, and an Australian file snake waited seven years.

Recent studies by Gordon Schuett et al.

During snake courtship and mating, the female generally remains passive, while the male moves around in a jerky, excited fashion.

suggest that reports of "exceptional cases of long-term sperm storage in female reptiles" should be re-examined, as production of embryos and offspring in at least four species of snakes apparently has resulted from parthenogenesis (reproduction without fertilization). Some species give birth to offspring every year, while others skip years and may not reproduce for some time. (Arafura file snakes, Shine says, only reproduce about once every ten years.)

For centuries, humans have marveled that male snakes possess paired sexual organs, yet scientists still aren't sure why serpents have two hemipenes, since only one is inserted into the female's cloaca at a time. One explanation is that the better-situated organ—the one closer to the female—is pressed into service. Based on his observations of kingsnakes, however, herpetologist Richard Zweifel suggests that while "randomness" may dominate after mating intervals of six days or more, alternation of the hemipenes is customary following intervals of up to three days.

When not in use, the hemipenes are retracted into the tail and kept inside out; when aroused (or squeezed by a herpetologist wishing to "sex" an individual), the male everts the organs, exposing a daunting array of sharp spines or hooks. These spines, which vary in shape and size from one species to the next, anchor the organ inside the female's cloaca while sperm is being transferred. Should either the female or male attempt to move away, the partner may end up being dragged along as well. On one such occasion, Harvey Lillywhite observed a male black racer dragging his mate 16 feet (5 m) up a tree.

After copulation, the snakes separate and go about their ways—which, for some males, means finding another female, thus

enhancing the odds of fathering more offspring.

Males of some species—garter snakes, for example—secrete a chemical that forms a "copulatory plug" that blocks successful mating with a female for up to three days. Male red-sided garter snakes also release a pheromone that creates "temporary impotence in other males if they linger too long in contact with the mated pair," Ernst and Zug report.

Since a female's pheromones, rather than her physical appearance or behavior, are the primary stimulant for the male, it is easy to understand why males sometimes attempt to mate with dead females. Shine recounts the astonishing story of a railsplitter in New South Wales who killed a large diamond snake in 1922 and, the following day, discovered a second diamond snake "coiled lovingly around the remains of the first." He killed that one too, and, in

Diamond carpet python crossbreed

During the spring mating season, Australian diamond pythons congregate in groups of a single adult female and up to four males. Diamond pythons interbreed readily with a subspecies, the carpet python, in captivity and in some areas of New South Wales.

"The first and chief quality of the snake—the sensation it excites in us—is its snakiness, our best word for a feeling compounded of many elements, not readily analysable, which has in it something of fear and something of the sense of mystery."
—W. H. Hudson,
The Book of a Naturalist, 1919

When it is time for snake eggs to hatch, baby snakes cut their way out with an "egg tooth" that slits the shell.

due time, a third and a fourth. When the odor of the "disintegrating serpents" grew unbearable, the rail-splitter decided to cremate them—but not before two more materialized and were added to the pyre.

Considerable interest has been generated by the curious fact that some snakes lay eggs, while others give birth to live young. Herpetologists call the egg layers "oviparous" and the live-bearers "viviparous"; sometimes the term "ovoviviparous" is substituted for the latter term in cases where the eggs retained in the female's oviduct either hatch inside or hatch immediately after extrusion. In some instances, a normally oviparous specimen such as a smooth green snake may not lay her eggs until just before hatching, or the offspring may even emerge before she deposits the shelled eggs. Unlike the relatively brittle eggs of birds, snake eggs are usually thick and leathery, but they are permeable to gases and likely to swell if they absorb water.

Females generally seek out private nesting sites in which to lay their eggs, such as beneath a rock or inside a decaying log, unused animal burrow, manure pile, sawdust heap, anthill, termite nest, or leaf litter, but a number of species (including milk snakes, black racers, and rat snakes) lay their eggs in communal nesting sites, perhaps due to a shortage of ideal nesting places.

Shine recalls the story of a surprised bulldozer operator in Queensland, Australia, who uncovered a clutch of more than five hundred eggs deposited by yellow-faced whipsnakes in a crack beneath a road. Since whipsnakes typically lay about six eggs, he calculated this giant incubation parlor represented the labors of nearly one hundred females. Among other species, the average clutch size varies considerably, from a single egg to the 104 found in a mud snake that had been killed on a Florida road. Live-bearers can produce even more, the record being held by a puff adder that gave birth to 156 young.

Eggs are commonly laid in sites that offer suitable warmth—from direct or indirect sunlight, or from decaying vegetation or manure—but a few species of snakes actually brood their eggs. The best known are the Indian python and carpet python, which coil around their eggs and raise their own body temperature slightly higher than the ambient air temperature by contracting their muscles.

In a few species, the eggs are attended by one or both adults; the most notorious of these, the king cobra, apparently form monogamous pairs. After mating, the female pushes or drags bamboo leaves and other vegetation to shape a nest with two compartments. The female then takes up residence in the compartment above the eggs, while the male, which is reportedly quite aggressive during this period, remains nearby.

When it is time for the eggs to hatch, the baby snakes cut their way out with an "egg tooth" that slits the shell. This tooth, generally shed within a few days of birth, can also be seen in live-born young, including rattlesnakes and copperheads.

Predation

"Though limbless, lethargic, and small-brained," Carr once observed, "the snake is one of the most perfectly efficient predators in the animal world." That assertion might come as something of a surprise to most people, who probably regard the absence of limbs—legs for chasing prey, and arms and hands for grabbing it and guid-

Water snake eating American toad
Above: *Water snakes consume large numbers of frogs, toads, fish, salamanders, and other small animals, which they swallow live and whole. This water snake chased an American toad at night for some distance along the bank of a creek before eventually catching and eating it.*

Green anaconda
Left: *Green anacondas of South America lie submerged in rivers and streams, where they ambush aquatic prey and animals that come to the water to drink. Anacondas are constrictors, grasping their victim and coiling around its body to compress the heart and cause circulatory arrest.*

Boa constrictor

The boa constrictor is a ground dweller whose bold skin pattern provides camouflage in the leaf litter of forests from Mexico to Argentina. Although they lack heat-sensitive pits, these snakes have sharp teeth and will patiently lie in ambush for small mammals and other vertebrate prey.

"From a rodent's point of view, a viper is a sort of demonic mousetrap."
—Thomas Palmer,
Landscape with Reptile: Rattlesnakes in an Urban World, 1992

ing it into the mouth—as a serious handicap.

But snakes have evolved a revolutionary physical design that compensates for their lack of limbs: elastic jaws, which expand to accommodate large prey; sharp, inwardly pointed teeth, to discourage live prey from escaping; large fangs at the front of the mouth, in some species, equipped to deliver venom, or, in other species, rear fangs grooved to channel venom into the tightly held prey; and a distensible throat and body that permit ingested prey to travel down into the stomach, where the digestive enzymes finish their work.

In general, snakes employ one of three principal methods of finding food: lying in wait to ambush prey that venture nearby; luring prey within striking range by waving a tail or tongue; or actively hunting and tracking their prey.

The superbly camouflaged timber rattle-snake, for example, often waits quietly beside a rodent's pathway, coiling behind a fallen log and resting its chin on the edge, where it can feel vibrations created by small mammals. Some newborn pit vipers, such as cottonmouths and copperheads, and a few other species wriggle the tips of their tails to lure prospective prey attracted to the contrasting bright yellow coloration, which suggests a grub or worm. Foraging species, on the other hand, stalk their prey by following chemical trails.

To overpower their quarry, many snakes strike and hold their prey in their mouth, relying on teeth and muscles to anchor the animal while the snake "walks" its expandable jaws over the live meal. On occasion, the muffled cries of a frog emanate from a snake's stomach, and sometimes the victim is regurgitated—dazed but still alive—when a snake is disturbed while swallowing.

Venomous serpents, of course, have evolved a more efficient method for subduing their prey: injecting venom into the victim's vital parts and waiting for it to become paralyzed or die. It is the constrictors, however—especially the well-publicized pythons and boas, as well as pine, bull, king, milk, and rat snakes—that fascinate and horrify at the same time.

"To most people," Carr writes, "constricting seems one of the more lurid and unpardonable things that snakes do. Though I come from an enlightened family, I grew up thinking that a constricting snake snatches its prey, throws on coils, and with chiropractic precision pulverizes each separate bone in its victim's body, licks the pulped prey all over to lubricate it, zestfully engulfs it, and then lays up somewhere for a year or more, stupefied by its excesses."

Not quite. Although some of these exaggerated maneuvers can be glimpsed in Hollywood movies like the ridiculous *Anaconda,* the act of constriction is rather more complex. To overcome their prey, constrictors do not simply "squeeze" a victim to death, as was once believed, crushing the bones into tiny pieces; while the occasional rib may be cracked in larger quarry, "such breaks are rare," Ernst and Zug report.

The tightening of a snake's coils, it has long been argued, can strangle or cause prevention of breathing in a victim, leading to asphyxiation (lack of oxygen) and suffocation (cessation of external respiration). But, as David L. Hardy, Sr., recently reported, circulatory arrest is the primary cause of death. In subduing prey, Hardy writes, "constricting snakes coil around the thoracic cage containing the heart and lungs. As the coils tighten, it appears the heart is compressed by the ribs and diaphragm . . . while the lungs are deflated." The result, he says, is interruption of the flow of blood and failure of cellular respiration of the heart muscle.

The prey consumed by these gapers, envenomators, and constrictors range in size from the very tiny (such as termites, whose abdomens are sucked out by thread snakes) to the giant (tapirs, antelopes, small leopards, and, in a handful of confirmed cases, humans). More commonly consumed are amphibians (such as frogs, toads, and salamanders), reptiles (including lizards and snakes, the latter being ideally shaped for consumption by other snakes), fish, birds and their eggs, and rodents. Smaller serpents also eat insects, slugs, snails, earthworms, and other invertebrates.

Some snakes are "generalists," eating whatever food happens to be available during a particular season or in a given habitat, while others are highly specialized and depend on a limited diet. These latter are the more vulnerable, particularly when humans destroy a microhabitat and wipe out a snake's vital food sources. All snakes are carnivorous and eat live food, but individuals devour roadkill on occasion, and many zoo specimens and pets can be induced to eat nonliving food, especially if it still generates body heat or has been rubbed with the scent of a favored prey.

After consuming a big meal, a snake may rest for a relatively long period of time before it requires more food. During a period of abstention, a large snake may go without food for six to twelve months at a time without significant loss of weight. Captive boas, bandy-bandys, and puff adders are all well known for their long fasting periods, and a rock python once went two years and nine months between meals.

*S*trings of rattlesnake rattles do *not* indicate the age of an individual snake, since one rattle is added every time the snake sheds its skin; long strings are subject to wear and tear in the wild and frequently break apart.

Hibernation

"Fall," wrote J. Frank Dobie in his popular book *Rattlesnakes*, "is the time when rattlesnakes change their dispositions." As they instinctively head toward their winter dens, some species tend to congregate. Early reports from the American West of giant "balls" of rattlesnakes were routinely discounted as tall tales until accounts by more reliable witnesses began to find their way into mainstream literature.

In September of 1898, for example, Dr. F. R. Seyffert was on medical call when he encountered several rattlesnakes at the edge of a gully. "When my attention was free," he told Dobie, "I looked over into the gully [and] saw a sight that literally froze my blood . . . a writhing, squirming mass of rattlesnakes, hundreds of them. . . . The twisted, twisting bola . . . was a solid mass of rattlesnake bodies, and rattlesnakes all around it were somehow entangling themselves with the bola. The snakes were not rattling; they were just crawling and writhing."

At the time, Dobie and others believed rattlesnakes mated only in the spring; today, field researchers know that fall matings are common as well. But the relation of the snake ball, or bola, to hibernation is an intriguing one: do rattlesnakes, whipsnakes, ring-necked snakes, red-bellied snakes, garter snakes, and others aggregate in winter dens to conserve heat or moisture, or because of a scarcity of underground quarters in which to escape freezing temperatures? Or do they aggregate so that males can locate females for mating in late fall or after emerging in the spring?

Whatever the case, hibernation is a physiological adaptation for surviving in habitats subjected to cold winter temperatures. Although given various labels—overwintering, winter sleep, dormancy, brumation, winter numbness, and winter inactivity—hibernation is the correct designation, Ernst and Zug affirm, since many hibernating reptiles "experience major physiological changes."

In snake hibernation chambers, or hibernacula, which are usually underground refuges, temperatures may range from about 40° to 52° F (4.5° to 11° C). In the United States, the average dormancy period may last only a few months a year, depending on the latitude and altitude, but in northern Canada, northern Asia, and central Europe, reptiles may hibernate five to seven months and as long as eight or nine months in some regions or mountain ranges. "It is astounding," Robert Mertens once remarked, "that a vertebrate can survive when the total period of its active life does not extend for more than three to four months!"

Many snakes retreat singly to subterranean crevices, animal burrows, anthills, root systems, and the like, where soil temperatures remain fairly stable even when air temperatures drop below freezing. Snakes that aggregate in winter dens may share their quarters with other species of snakes, and sometimes other animals as well. In Queensland, Australia, after a bulldozer knocked over a dead tree in winter, out writhed thirty or forty brown tree snakes, green tree snakes, and carpet pythons ("like spaghetti in a bad dream," the driver reported afterward).

Because the young are often born in late summer, some have to locate winter dens fairly quickly. Although older snakes may use celestial or solar cues, landmarks, or olfactory cues, researchers have found that

*S*nakes can be found today virtually everywhere on Earth, except for the continent of Antarctica and the islands of Iceland, Greenland, Ireland, and New Zealand.

some newborns follow a scent trail left by their mothers. Neonate (newborn) timber rattlesnakes, for example, follow a pheromone trail on the substrate left by adults and other siblings and may even be following their own fathers.

In the United States, one of the most famous of all snake dens is near Murphysboro in southern Illinois, overlooking the Mississippi River. Here, Marlin Perkins, then curator of reptiles at the St. Louis Zoological Park, would escort prominent herpetologists in the fall and spring to witness (and catch) an astonishing assortment of snakes in the vicinity of their winter dens. Today, this area of the Shawnee National Forest is celebrated for its seasonal migrations of snakes between the swampland and the limestone bluffs, and for several weeks every spring and fall the U.S. Forest Service closes off the narrow road to all vehicular traffic.

Like many amphibians, most temperate-zone reptiles are able to survive brief periods of "supercooling," according to Zug, but freezing "is lethal to all but a few species." For snakes, winter hibernation is not a period of deep sleep; instead, snakes "move deeper, episodically, as outside temperatures decline, remaining stationary only when temperatures are near or below freezing," Ernst and Zug explain. Later, as external temperatures begin to rise, the snakes "gradually shift toward the entrance," periodically emerging to bask if temperatures rise earlier than usual and eventually leaving once the days lengthen and the ground begins to warm.

In parts of the world where conditions are especially dry, snakes will estivate—that is, retreat below ground during the hottest period—to conserve body moisture and protect their bodies from extreme temperatures. These species usually burrow into mud or soil and encase themselves in hardened balls of dried earth; some, however, move into deserted animal burrows or hollow trees. Strangely enough, desert-dwelling species do not estivate, herpetologist Hubert Saint-Girons says, probably because they "may be better adapted to heat."

Timber rattlesnake

Some snakes hibernate individually, while others share communal winter dens (hibernacula) where temperatures are low but remain above freezing. Timber rattlesnakes once congregated in rocky crevices in groups of one hundred or more, but overzealous hunters have decimated their numbers; these snakes are now nearly extinct in some parts of their range.

Key to Scientific Names

Although herpetologists customarily refer to snakes by their scientific names, the public generally uses one or more common names for the same serpents. The following key has been prepared for readers who wish to determine the scientific names of species and subspecies referred to in the text.

Adder, European (*Vipera berus*)
Adder, horned (*Bitis caudalis*)
Adder, Peringuey's (*Bitis peringueyi*)
Adder, puff (*Bitis arietans*)
Adder, rhinoceros (*Bitis nasicornis*)
Aesculapian snake (*Elaphe longissima*)
Anacondas (*Eunectes*)
Anaconda, green (*Eunectes murinus*)

Bandy-bandy (*Vermicella annulata*)
Black-headed snakes (*Tantilla*)
Black-striped snakes (*Coniophanes*)
Blackhood snake (*Tantilla rubra cucullata*)
Blacksnakes, Australian (*Pseudechis*)
Blind snakes (*Ramphotyphlops, Leptotyphlops*)
Blind snake, Brahminy (*Ramphotyphlops braminus*)
Boa, Brazilian rainbow (*Epicrates cenchria cenchria*)
Boa, Colombian rainbow (*Epicrates cenchria maurus*)
Boa, Dumeril's (*Boa dumerili*)
Boa, emerald tree (*Corallus caninus*)
Boa, Hog Island (*Boa constrictor sabogae*)
Boa, Madagascan tree (*Boa mandrita*)
Boa, Mona (*Epicrates monensis monensis*)
Boa, Pacific tree (*Candoia bibronii*)
Boa, Pacific viper (*Candoia aspera*)
Boa, Puerto Rican (*Epicrates inornatus*)
Boa, rainbow (*Epicrates cenchria*)
Boa, Round Island tree (*Casarea dussumieri*)
Boa, Virgin Islands tree (*Epicrates monensis granti*)
Boa constrictor (*Boa constrictor*)
Boomslang (*Dispholidus typus*)
Brown snake (*Storeria dekayi*)
Brownsnake, Australian eastern (*Pseudonaja textilis*)
Bullsnake (*Pituophis catenifer sayi*)
Bushmaster (*Lachesis muta*)

Cascabel (*Crotalus durissus*)
Cat snake, green (*Boiga cyanea*)
Cat-eyed snake, Northern (*Leptodeira septentrionalis*)

Coachwhip snake (*Masticophis flagellum*)
Cobra, black-necked spitting (*Naja nigricollis*)
Cobra, Chinese (*Naja atra*)
Cobra, coral (*Aspidelaps lubricus*)
Cobra, Egyptian (*Naja haje*)
Cobra, Indian (*Naja naja*)
Cobra, Javan (*Naja sputatrix*)
Cobra, king (*Ophiophagus hannah*)
Cobra, monocled (*Naja kaouthia*)
Cobra, Mozambique spitting (*Naja mossambica*)
Cobra, shield-nosed (*Aspidelaps scutatus*)
Cobra, Siamese (*Naja siamensis*)
Cobra, Sumatran (*Naja sumatranus*)
Copperhead (*Agkistrodon contortrix*)
Copperhead, Australian (*Austrelaps superbus*)
Copperhead, broad-banded (*Agkistrodon contortrix laticinctus*)
Copperhead, Northern (*Agkistrodon contortrix mokasen*)
Copperhead, Osage (*Agkistrodon contortrix phaeogaster*)
Copperhead, Southern (*Agkistrodon contortrix contortrix*)
Copperhead, Trans-Pecos (*Agkistrodon contortrix pictigaster*)
Coral snake (*Micrurus fulvius*)
Coral snake, Eastern (*Micrurus fulvius fulvius*)
Corn snake (*Elaphe guttata*)
Cottonmouth (*Agkistrodon piscivorus*)
Crowned snake, Southeastern (*Tantilla coronata*)

DeKay's snake (*Storeria dekayi dekayi*)

Earth snakes (*Virginia*)

Fer-de-lance (*Bothrops asper*)
File snakes (*Acrochordus*)
File snake, Arafura (*Acrochordus arafurae*)
Flathead snake (*Tantilla gracilis*)
Flowerpot snake (*Ramphotyphlops braminus*)
Flying snake (*Chrysopelia ornata*)
Fox snake (*Elaphe vulpina*)

Garter snakes (*Thamnophis*)
Garter snake, checkered (*Thamnophis marcianus*)

Garter snake, Chicago (*Thamnophis sirtalis semifasciatus*)
Garter snake, common (*Thamnophis sirtalis*)
Garter snake, Eastern (*Thamnophis sirtalis sirtalis*)
Garter snake, giant (*Thamnophis gigas*)
Garter snake, Northwestern (*Thamnophis ordinoides*)
Garter snake, plains (*Thamnophis radix*)
Garter snake, red-sided (*Thamnophis sirtalis parietalis*)
Garter snake, San Francisco (*Thamnophis sirtalis infernalis*)
Garter snake, wandering (*Thamnophis elegans vagrans*)
Gopher snake (*Pituophis catenifer*)
Grass snake (*Natrix natrix*)
Green snake, rough (*Opheodrys aestivus*)
Green snake, smooth (*Liochlorophis vernalis*)

Halloween snakes (*Pliocercus*)
Hog-nosed snake, Eastern (*Heterodon platirhinos*)
Hog-nosed snake, Southern (*Heterodon simus*)
Hog-nosed snake, Western (*Heterodon nasicus*)
Hooknose snakes (*Gyalopion, Ficimia*)

Indigo snake, Eastern (*Drymarchon corais couperi*)

Kingsnakes (*Lampropeltis*)
Kingsnake, Blair's (*Lampropeltis mexicana blairi*)
Kingsnake, California (*Lampropeltis getula californiae*)
Kingsnake, California mountain (*Lampropeltis zonata*)
Kingsnake, common (*Lampropeltis getula*)
Kingsnake, gray-banded (*Lampropeltis alterna*)
Kingsnake, scarlet (*Lampropeltis triangulum elapsoides*)
Kingsnake, speckled (*Lampropeltis getula holbrooki*)
Kingsnake, Thayer's (*Lampropeltis mexicana thayeri*)
Krait, banded (*Bungarus fasciatus*)

Lancehead, golden (*Bothrops insularis*)

Lyre snakes (*Trimorphodon*)

Mamba, black (*Dendroaspis polylepis*)
Mamba, green (*Dendroaspis angusticeps*)
Mamba, Jameson's (*Dendroaspis jamesoni*)
Mamba, West African green (*Dendroaspis viridis*)
Mangrove snake (*Boiga dendrophila*)
Massasauga (*Sistrurus catenatus*)
Milk snake (*Lampropeltis triangulum*)
Milk snake, Blanchard's (*Lampropeltis triangulum blanchardi*)
Milk snake, Central Plains (*Lampropeltis triangulum gentilis*)
Milk snake, Eastern (*Lampropeltis triangulum triangulum*)
Milk snake, Honduran (*Lampropeltis triangulum hondurensis*)
Milk snake, Louisiana (*Lampropeltis triangulum amaura*)
Milk snake, Mexican (*Lampropeltis triangulum annulata*)
Milk snake, red (*Lampropeltis triangulum syspila*)
Milk snake, Sinoloan (*Lampropeltis triangulum sinaloae*)
Montpellier snake (*Malpolon monspessulanus*)
Mud snake (*Farancia abacura*)
Mud snake, Eastern (*Farancia abacura abacura*)
Mud snake, Western (*Farancia abacura reinwardtii*)

Parrot snakes (*Leptophis*)
Pine snake, Eastern (*Pituophis melanoleucas*)
Pipe snakes (*Cylindrophis*)
Pit viper, Malayan (*Calloselasma rhodostoma*)
Pit viper, McGregor's (*Trimeresurus mcgregori*)
Python, African rock (*Python sebae*)
Python, Asian rock (*Python molurus*)
Python, black-headed (*Aspidites melanocephalus*)
Python, blood (*Python curtus*)
Python, Burmese (*Python molurus bivittatus*)
Python, carpet (*Morelia spilota*)
Python, diamond (*Morelia spilota spilota*)
Python, green tree (*Morelia viridis*)
Python, Indian (*Python molurus*)
Python, Oenpelli (*Morelia oenpelliensis*)
Python, reticulated (*Python reticulatus*)

Racer, black (*Coluber constrictor constrictor*)
Rainbow snake (*Farancia erytrogramma*)
Rat snakes (*Elaphe*)
Rat snake, black (*Elaphe obsoleta obsoleta*)

Rat snake, Everglades (*Elaphe obsoleta rossalleni*)
Rat snake, Great Plains (*Elaphe emoryi*)
Rat snake, Japanese (*Elaphe climacophora*)
Rat snake, red-tailed green (*Gonyosoma oxycephala*)
Rat snake, Texas (*Elaphe obsoleta lindheimerii*)
Rat snake, yellow (*Elaphe obsoleta quadrivittata*)
Rattlesnake, black-tailed (*Crotalus molossus*)
Rattlesnake, canebrake (*Crotalus horridus atricaudatus*)
Rattlesnake, Carolina pigmy (*Sistrurus miliarius miliarius*)
Rattlesnake, dusky pigmy (*Sistrurus miliarius barbouri*)
Rattlesnake, Eastern diamondback (*Crotalus adamanteus*)
Rattlesnake, Mojave (*Crotalus scutulatus*)
Rattlesnake, New Mexico ridge-nosed (*Crotalus willardi obscurus*)
Rattlesnake, pigmy (*Sistrurus miliarius*)
Rattlesnake, red diamond (*Crotalus ruber*)
Rattlesnake, tiger (*Crotalus tigris*)
Rattlesnake, timber (*Crotalus horridus*)
Rattlesnake, Western (*Crotalus viridis*)
Rattlesnake, Western diamondback (*Crotalus atrox*)
Rattlesnake, Western pigmy (*Sistrurus miliarius streckeri*)
Red-bellied snake (*Storeria occipitomaculata*)
Red-bellied snake, Northern (*Storeria occipitomaculata occipitomaculata*)
Ribbon snake, Eastern (*Thamnophis sauritus sauritus*)
Ribbon snake, Western (*Thamnophis proximus proximus*)
Ring-necked snake (*Diadophis punctatus*)
Ring-necked snake, Northern (*Diadophis punctatus edwardsii*)
Ring-necked snake, Southern (*Diadophis punctatus punctatus*)
Rinkhals, African (*Hemachatus haemachatus*)

Salt marsh snake, Atlantic (*Nerodia clarkii taeniata*)
Scarlet snake (*Cemophora coccinea*)
Sea krait, banded (*Laticauda semifasciata*)
Sea krait, yellow-lipped (*Laticauda colubrina*)
Sea snake, olive (*Aipysurus laevis*)
Sea snake, yellow-bellied (*Pelamis platurus*)
Sidewinder (*Crotalus cerastes*)
Sunbeam snakes (*Xenopeltis*)

Taipan (*Oxyuranus scutellatus*)
Taipan, inland (*Oxyuranus microlepidotus*)
Tentacled snake (*Erpeton tentaculatus*)
Tiger snake, neotropical (*Spilotes pullatus*)
Tree snake, banded (*Tripanurgos compressus*)
Tree snake, brown (*Boiga irregularis*)
Twig snakes (*Thelotornis*)
Twig snake, savanna (*Thelotornis capensis*)

Vine snakes (*Ahaetulla, Oxybelis, Xenoxybelis*)
Vine snake, Asian (*Ahaetulla nasuta*)
Vine snake, brown (*Oxybelis aeneus*)
Vine snake, Madagascan (*Langaha nasuta*)
Viper, African (*Causus rhombeatus*)
Viper, eyelash (*Bothriechis schlegelii*)
Viper, Gaboon (*Bitis gabonica*)
Viper, horned (*Cerastes cerastes*)
Viper, island pit (*Trimeresurus labialis*)
Viper, jumping (*Atropoides nummifer*)
Viper, Macmahon's (*Eristicophis macmahoni*)
Viper, rhinoceros (*Bitis nasicornis*)
Viper, Russell's (*Daboia russelli*)
Viper, sand (*Cerastes vipera*)
Viper, saw-scaled (*Echis carinatus*)
Viper, two-striped forest pit (*Bothriopsis bilineata*)

Water moccasin (*Agkistrodon piscivorus*)
Water snakes (*Nerodia*)
Water snake, Concho (*Nerodia harteri paucimaculata*)
Water snake, diamondback (*Nerodia rhombifer*)
Water snake, Florida green (*Nerodia floridana*)
Water snake, Northern (*Nerodia sipedon sipedon*)
Water snake, plainbelly (*Nerodia erythrogaster*)
Water snake, red-bellied (*Nerodia erythrogaster erythrogaster*)
Water snake, Southern (*Nerodia fasciata*)
Whipsnakes (*Masticophis*)
Whipsnake, Alameda (*Masticophis lateralis euryzanthus*)
Whipsnake, yellow-faced (*Demansia psammophis*)
Worm snake (*Carphophis amoenus*)
Worm snake, Eastern (*Carphophis amoenus amoenus*)
Worm snake, Midwest (*Carphophis amoenus helenae*)
Worm snake, Western (*Carphophis vermis*)

Families and Species

Green tree python
Facing page: *The word "python" is derived from the Greek word for "rotting serpent corpse."*

Burmese python
Inset: *Burmese pythons are relatively gentle and are prized as pets. An 8-foot specimen kept by herpetologist Clifford H. Pope in his suburban home near Chicago once disappeared, only to turn up later in the box springs of a bed. Pope's wife, who had napped on the mattress, recalled experiencing a "sleepy hallucination."*

Today, as in the 1700s, when Swedish taxonomist Carolus Linnaeus lumped reptiles and amphibians together into a "queer assembly" of "foul and loathsome" beasts he called *Amphibia,* there is considerable confusion regarding their classification. Herpetologists often disagree among themselves and engage in spirited public debate over nomenclature and classification of species and subspecies. As Shine succinctly put it, "The classification of snakes is a mess."

Historically, the class Amphibia and the class Reptilia have been studied together—despite the fact that "reptiles are no more closely related to amphibians than they are to mammals," according to Pough—because both groups are ectotherms. The living amphibians comprise three major groups: (1) frogs and toads; (2) salamanders and newts; and (3) caecilians (limbless burrowing creatures). The living reptiles comprise four major groups: (1) turtles; (2) crocodilians; (3) snakes and lizards; and (4) tuatara (lizardlike animals found on offshore islands of New Zealand).

Traditionally, snakes and lizards have been treated as distinct categories, but, as Pough notes, "in an evolutionary sense, the animals known as snakes are specialized lizards," and they are "coequal suborders" of the order Squamata (the "scaly reptiles"). Amphisbaenia—the third suborder of squamates—includes some 133 species of snakelike reptiles popularly known as worm-lizards or ringed lizards.

Of the approximately 6,700 living species of squamates, more than 2,700 are recognized species of snakes, Greene calculates. Scientists generally assign these species to twelve (but sometimes fifteen, seventeen, or eighteen) families, of which Colubridae is by far the largest, with more than 1,800 species. This family, known as the colubrids, "is sometimes called a 'trash-can group,'" Ernst and Zug declare, "because it contains many unrelated subgroups that are thrown together because biologists cannot decide where else to classify them." Most snakes native to the United States are colubrids, except for coral snakes (which belong to the family Elapidae, which also includes cobras, mambas, and kraits) and pit vipers (the rattlesnakes, copperheads, and cottonmouths, which belong to a subfamily of the family Viperidae).

Scientists believe the first snakes appeared sometime between 100 and 150 million years ago. Due to the fragility of snake skeletons, however, the fossil record for serpents is relatively poor. The oldest known fossil of a snake is an Algerian species dating back approximately 120 million years, according to Shine.

In 1997, after re-examining a pair of 97-million-year-old marine fossils formerly classified as lizards, paleontologists Michael Caldwell and Michael Lee reported that there is "compelling evidence" that primitive snakes once had legs. Both specimens of *Pachyrhachis prolematicus*, which had been found twenty years earlier in limestone quarries north of Jerusalem on the West Bank, were about 3 feet long (1 m) and equipped with a pelvis and short hind limbs. Interestingly, Caldwell and Lee's conclusion that these primitive snakes are of aquatic ancestry runs contrary to the prevailing hypothesis that snakes evolved from small burrowing lizards.

"All modern and fossil snakes share a common ancestor" with a group of marine lizards called mosasauroids, Caldwell told the *New York Times*, "but we don't know how far back that is. As for the question of when snakes lost their limbs, that one is still up for grabs."

Today, snakes can be found virtually everywhere on Earth, except for the continent of Antarctica and the islands of Iceland, Greenland, Ireland, and New Zealand. While some species may exclusively inhabit a single tiny island, others are distributed across far-reaching geographic territories. From sea level to altitudes of 16,000 feet (4,900 m), and as far from the equator as the Arctic Circle and the tip of South America, serpents have adapted extremely well to the world around them. In fact, they can be found in a remarkable array of habitats: tropical and temperate forests, grasslands, swamps, deserts, mountains, oceans and freshwater, even urban areas.

Nearly all snakes inhabit a "habitat niche"—an environment or range that reflects a preferred type of climate, food supply, terrain, and vegetation. Within this habitat, some species or individuals are primarily fossorial (burrowing beneath the ground), terrestrial, arboreal, semiaquatic, or aquatic. Others, however, readily shift between several realms.

Since individual snakes and other animals "wander and drift and are blown about the globe," Carr points out, they occasionally take up residence in new habitats and geographical ranges. The occasional migration of snakes, along with their generally secretive nature, hampers observation and poses a challenge for herpetolo-

The first snakes appeared between 100 and 150 million years ago.

gists trying to map habitats. Because it is so difficult to find snakes in some regions, "maps that show their distribution may have more to do with the distribution of herpetologists than with the snakes," reflects Mattison. Perhaps as a result, most volumes today (including this book) exclude range maps.

While serpents may be elusive, assumptions that they are "solitary and asocial," says Howard K. Reinert, are "probably inaccurate." Over the past thirty years, radiotelemetry—the surgical implantation of tiny transmitters into the body cavity—has permitted field biologists to study patterns of activity and distributions of certain species with much greater precision. Sometimes these field studies reveal unexpected seasonal aggregations of species, unforeseen habitat diversity, and nongeneralizable idiosyncracies of individuals.

Of the world's dozen or more families of snakes, the following portfolio showcases representative examples of widely recognized as well as unfamiliar or unusual species, including specimens from North America, Central and South America, Asia, Africa, and Australia.

Pythons and Boas
Burmese Python
Python molurus bivittatus

In 1945, herpetologist Clifford H. Pope was introduced to a python that had been discovered behind an Army mess hall in Burma and brought to the Field Museum of Natural History in Chicago, where he worked. Because it was difficult to keep the snake warm during the winter, Pope took "Sylvia" home to suburban Winnetka and settled her into his basement near the furnace.

Sylvia was to achieve considerable rep-

tilian celebrity—first among Pope's neighbors, and later among readers of *Life* magazine and his 1951 book *The Giant Snakes*, which he dedicated to her. But long before most Americans learned about Sylvia's lifestyle, officials down at the Winnetka Village Hall became aware of something unusual.

"After Sylvia had been with us for some time," Pope recalled, "we heard of steps the Village Hall had taken to warn meter readers and others. On our card in its files was a brief notation: 'Snake in basement.'"

Sylvia was about 8 feet long (2.44 m) at the time and a splendid example of human-snake coexistence. Burmese pythons, which are a subspecies of the Indian or Asian rock python, have long been popular in zoos, circuses, and burlesque shows because of their impressive size, colorful patterns, and relatively gentle disposition. Reaching lengths of up to 26 feet (7.92 m), Burmese pythons are found in the swamps, grasslands, and rocky foothills of Southeast Asia and the East Indies.

At one time, Indian pythons were thought to exist in two distinct color phases: a larger and darker variety, from Burma (now Myanmar) and the East Indies, and a paler gray or dark tan variety, with a pinkish head, from western India and Sri Lanka. The former is now commonly referred to as the Burmese python, the latter as the Indian python.

Burmese pythons typically sport a tan, yellow brown, or gray ground color with reddish to dark brown quadrangular blotches outlined in gold or cream. On the head is a dark spear-shaped marking. Other distinguishing physical characteristics include small iridescent scales, catlike pupils, and two spurs on the lower part of the body. Specimens are easily bred in captiv-

*B*urmese pythons may be as long as 26 feet (7.92 m)

Emerald tree boa

Right: *Emerald tree boas of the Amazon Basin are equipped with huge fanglike front teeth, which they employ to snare birds and other prey. These tree boas are believed to have difficulty ingesting their food unless they hang downwards while swallowing.*

Juvenile emerald tree boa

Below: *Unlike their brilliant-green parents, newborn emerald tree boas are usually yellow or reddish orange, sometimes even pink or blue green. As a juvenile matures, flecks of green gradually appear and cover the base color.*

than two months later, sport colors quite different from the adults: bright lemon yellow, gold, red, orange, or brown, offset with short bars or spots of purple and blue. The change to lime green, at about two years of age, can occur quite rapidly, Shine reports, although the reason for the abrupt transformation isn't clear. The brightly colored tails of some juveniles are reportedly used as lures for prey.

Like the emerald tree boa, this snake has elongated front teeth for snaring its food, and it is equipped with heat-sensitive pits on each side of its head—on the top jaw only—which can detect the presence of birds and other animals at a distance of up to 1 foot 6 inches (45.7 cm).

When disturbed, green tree pythons can be aggressive, Raymond Hoser says, "often biting seemingly without provocation. Due to their large, sharp teeth, their bites can be painful and usually draw blood." Humans sometimes bite back, however, and in New Guinea, natives consider them a delicacy.

Emerald Tree Boa
Corallus caninus

The emerald tree boa, an almost exclusively arboreal denizen of the Amazon Basin, has been characterized by herpetologist Angus Bellairs as "one of the most beautiful of all snakes." Sporting a brilliant emerald green base color patterned with white or yellow bands or spots down the middle of its back and a lemon yellow underside, this snake is superbly adapted to the ecological demands of its rain forest existence. The emerald green blends in well with the rain forest canopy, and the white crossbands or flecks (called disruptive coloration) enhance the snake's camouflage and make it virtually invisible to predators, humans,

and unsuspecting prey.

The cryptic effect extends to the snake's characteristic roosting position, identical to that of the green tree python: gripping a tree limb with its prehensile tail, the snake drapes its coils symmetrically first over one side, then the other. When completed, this compact bundle of loops not only stabilizes the snake but looks somewhat like a bunch of unripened bananas.

Unlike their tree python counterparts, which hatch from eggs, young emerald tree boas are live-born in litters of up to twenty. Offspring of both species, however, share unusual colorations markedly different from those of adults: brick or rusty red, dull orange, bright yellow, pinkish, or bluish green, patterned with white markings and dark purple or green borders. After several months, juveniles begin to turn the adult shade of brilliant green.

Emerald tree boas seldom exceed 4 feet (1.2 m), but some have been known to grow up to 6½ feet (2 m). Longer boas and pythons are more likely to be terrestrial, thus avoiding the challenge of balancing and anchoring their heavier bodies on arboreal perches. Reportedly, emerald tree boas are such agile climbers they can scale a vertical bamboo pole.

Situated along this snake's upper and lower lips are well-developed thermoreceptive pits, sensitive to very slight changes in temperature, which help the snake to locate prey and direct its strike. Equipped with huge, fanglike front teeth, these nocturnal snakes can seize and hang onto a variety of birds, lizards, squirrels, and bats, penetrating feathers or fur while maintaining a secure grip. Curiously, emerald tree boas seem to have difficulty ingesting their food unless they hang downward from a branch while swallowing.

Emerald tree boas are such agile climbers they can scale a vertical bamboo pole.

Notwithstanding their imposing teeth, these tree boas are reputed to be the "gentlest" of the three or four recognized species of *Corallus*. Their range, herpetologist Robert Henderson reports, is restricted to lowland tropical rain forests from northern South America and Brazil through Peru, Ecuador, and Bolivia.

Rainbow Boa
Epicrates cenchria

When D. H. Lawrence described an English rainbow ("a band of faint iridescence formed itself . . . [and] gleamed fiercely; steadily the colour gathered, mysteriously . . . til it arched indomitable") in his novel *The Rainbow*, he could just as easily have been describing a rainbow boa. His imagery conveys the same sense of wonder one feels when glimpsing the magical iridescence of this handsome serpent.

The Brazilian rainbow boa, one of nine or ten subspecies of rainbow boa, appears metallic blue or blue green, a color observers liken to the magnificent sheen of the morpho butterfly in Central America. In just the right sunlight, the snake's skin shimmers with a sparkling iridescence; these hues are not the true color of the snake, however, which is actually a mix of dull brown, red, orange, black, and white, patterned with ringlike blotches, or eyespots.

"Iridescent colors can only be permanent if the tissue structures that produce them remain unchanged," explains authority Hilda Simon. "Because they constantly change their skins, shedding the old one and growing new layers underneath the old, reptiles cannot have any permanent iridescent colors." Prior to shedding, the smooth scales become a striking silvery white.

Nonetheless, the startling effect of the iridescence, combined with the imposing head and striking vertical pupils, has inspired a number of baseless horror stories about this nocturnal snake. In reality rainbow boas are quite harmless, and many Central and South American natives keep them as pets.

Rainbow boas have fairly heavy bodies and large heads; they seldom exceed 4 feet (1.22 m), though they occasionally reach 7 feet (2.13 m). Females bear eight to twenty live young. Ranging from Costa Rica southward through the Amazon Basin to Argentina and Paraguay, these snakes favor tropical forests and savannas and are one of the most common species of boa in Amazonia. Feeding principally on rodents and birds, they turn up from time to time in villages and on plantations, attracted by poultry and rodents.

Colombian rainbow boa
Above: *One of nine or ten subspecies of rainbow boa, the Colombian rainbow boa generally grows drabber in color as it ages. Like all rainbow boas, however, its skin displays a gleaming blue green iridescence when the scales catch the light.*

Brazilian rainbow boa
Facing page: *Although an agile climber, the relatively slow-moving Brazilian rainbow boa spends much of its time on the ground, where it hunts rodents and occasionally forages for chickens on farms near tropical forests.*

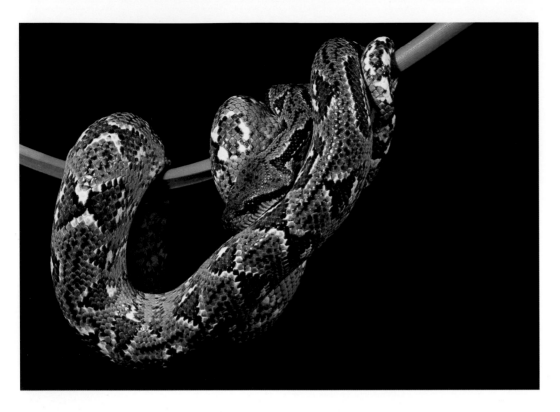

Madagascan tree boa
The Madagascan tree boa is one of three species of boas native to the island of Madagascar, where it lives in tropical rain forests.

Male Madagascan tree boas sometimes spar with one another and spur each other with their suspended lower bodies while lying in coils on tree limbs.

Madagascan Tree Boa
Boa mandrita

The tree boas of Madagascar, like a number of other animals on this island off the east coast of Africa, look so much like their counterparts on the South American continent that they were once assigned to a New World genus. Like emerald tree boas and green tree pythons, Madagascan tree boas are an entirely different color at birth, typically bright red or reddish brown. As the young snakes mature, they gradually assume the adult coloration and pattern: an olive green or tannish brown ground color, with dark brown spots or blotches shaped like a bow tie, bordered with white.

"No totally satisfactory explanation has been proposed for this remarkable convergence involving as it does species from South America, Australasia and Madagascar," observes Mattison. "Each of the species concerned is arboreal, but each is rather bulkier than most other arboreal snakes. The most likely explanation is that the colour change corresponds to change in habit, with young snakes perhaps occupying different positions within the forest canopy." Curiously, female Madagascan tree boas become darker when pregnant, "presumably to optimize the absorption of radiation and thus speed up the development of their embryos," Mattison speculates.

Found in tropical rain forests throughout most of Madagascar, these tree boas average 6 to 7 feet (1.83 to 2.13 m) but are known to reach lengths of 8 feet 3 inches (2.5 m). Males, according to Greene, sometimes spar with one another and "spur each other with their suspended lower bodies while lying in adjacent coils on tree limbs." In their arboreal habitat, tree boas prey chiefly on birds and small mammals.

Heavy deforestation threatens Madagascan tree boas with extinction, and in 1977 they were classified as endangered. Although they can no longer be traded, smuggling remains a serious problem, and a federal grand jury in Florida recently indicted six persons for conspiracy to smuggle hundreds of rare reptiles into the United States from Madagascar—including ninety-four Madagascan tree boas.

North American Nonvenomous Snakes
Green Snakes
Smooth Green Snake
(*Liochlorophis vernalis*)
Rough Green Snake
(*Opheodrys aestivus*)

My first encounter with a snake came at the age of eight in a Chicago alley. True, the alley was in a North Shore suburb, but the chance meeting was startling nonetheless: I was alone, as was the snake, and to this day I don't know which of us was the more surprised. The slender serpent turned out to be a smooth green snake, a gorgeous leaf-green species more mild-mannered than any snake I have met since. Because of our encounter, I became fascinated with snakes and wanted to learn more about them. I suspect now that if this handsome serpent had been an ill-tempered water snake or foul-smelling garter snake, this volume would never have been written.

That such a small creature (it was barely longer than a foot) could have such an impact may sound strange, but there's something about a green snake that invites a special feeling. Harmonizing with surrounding shrubbery and vines, this snake's delicate green coloration is so beautiful, its satiny skin so smooth, and its dark round iris so unthreatening, it provides an ideal introduction to the world of reptiles.

The extraordinary eyes of some snakes suggest "intelligence," and, if nothing else, the large eyes of green snakes give them an especially alert look. The specimen photographed for this book demonstrated its alertness while ensconced on my desk at the university: whenever a new screen-saver image materialized on my computer, the motion on the screen commanded the curious snake's attention.

Rarely exceeding 20 inches (51 cm) in length—the record is 26 inches (66 cm)—smooth green snakes are found from southern Canada to the Gulf of Mexico and from the Atlantic Ocean west to the

Rough green snake
The rough green snake is a superb climber, concealing itself among vines, stems, and other greenery, where it "freezes" in position for long periods of time to avoid detection.

*G*reen snakes are a gardener's best friend, devouring crickets, grasshoppers, spiders, snails, slugs, centipedes, and hairless caterpillars.

Rough green snake

North American green snakes are handsome and quite harmless creatures, distinguished by their delicate pale green coloration, striking black iris, and alert expression. This specimen, while waiting to be photographed, was fascinated by the rotating screen-saver scenes on the author's computer monitor.

Rocky Mountains. Unlike the rough green snake, the smooth species is predominantly a ground dweller, although it, too, is occasionally glimpsed in low bushes. This snake forages by day in grasses and other vegetation, looking for insects. In fact, the green snake is a gardener's best friend, devouring crickets, grasshoppers, spiders, snails, slugs, centipedes, and hairless caterpillars.

Green snakes hibernate during the winter, often alone but sometimes communally, and one of the most amazing reports of snake aggregation relates to this species. In the fall of 1934, a farmer noticed two smooth green snakes beside an anthill on his property in Treesbank, Manitoba. After he began digging up the anthill, roughly 6 inches (15.2 cm) high and 3 feet (0.91 m) in diameter, he discovered several lower "galleries" that he said were "alive with snakes." After several more days of digging, the farmer tallied up his serpentine inven-

tory and announced he had found 148 smooth green snakes, 101 red-bellied snakes, and 8 plains garter snakes, for a grand total of 257 snakes.

The rough green snake, whose classification into as many as four subspecies (Eastern, Western, Florida, and barrier islands) remains controversial, is distinguished from its smooth ally by its keeled scales and longer, tapering tail. Averaging about 2 to 3 feet (61 to 91 cm) but achieving a record 45⅝ inches (115.9 cm), the rough green snake sports similar green coloration on its back but usually has a sulfur-yellow or cream-colored underside (the smooth species ordinarily has a pale white belly). Ranging from southern New Jersey to the Florida Keys and west to Kansas and Oklahoma, the rough green snake is an arboreal creature, found in thickets or fields and in shrubs or trees overhanging lakes or streams. Blackberry patches, hummocks, pastures, and drainage ditches are other favorite habitats. In residential areas, they are sometimes killed by lawn mowers or found dead on the road, where their green coloration turns blue, just as it does in formaldehyde.

Like smooth green snakes, rough green snakes are active by day and sleep at night, sometimes lying on horizontal perches 5 feet (1.5 m) or higher among the branches of trees or tall shrubs and resting their head on a body coil. By day, this snake relies on its green coloration for camouflage, which may explain why these snakes are generally sighted on bare dirt or pavement, where their otherwise "invisible" coloration is more conspicuous.

When encountered by humans or predators (domestic cats, for example), a rough green snake often freezes in position; if provoked, however, it will dart toward the nearest vegetation and disappear in a flash, making further pursuit fruitless. Anyone cunning enough to sneak up on a green snake will discover that most do not bite—especially smooth green snakes. Rough green snakes may make a feeble effort to bite, but this is likely a gaping behavior that displays the darker lining of the mouth.

Recent studies utilizing radio transmitters implanted in females indicate that rough green snakes return to former nesting sites to lay their eggs. Herpetologist Michael Plummer has located some nests in hollow trees as high as 9 feet 9 inches (3 m) off the ground—a surprising discovery, since green snakes traditionally were believed to deposit their eggs beneath flat rocks or in rotting stumps and logs. Clutches of eggs are usually laid in late summer and consist of two to fourteen thin, leathery, adhesive eggs. Vivid emerald green hatchlings emerge three to four weeks later.

Black Racer
Coluber constrictor

The black racer is a snake with attitude.

"It is a bold and daring serpent," one naturalist declared a century ago, warning that it enters barns and outhouses "without fear." Once, while walking through a cottonfield, Raymond Ditmars encountered a black racer (or black snake, as it was then commonly called) that grew enraged when its escape route was blocked; after thrashing about hysterically, it confronted its pursuer. It was the "maddest snake" he had ever seen, Ditmars recalled, and it struck at him "a dozen times."

Carl Kauffeld remembers a black racer that caught at his pants leg while he was walking along an embankment in Florida. When he glanced down, there was a 3½-foot (1.07-m) black racer "lashing at me in long lunges." Though amused at first, Kauffeld soon tired of its behavior and "flung him as far as I could." But within minutes, the snake was back, "renewing the attack with unabated fury."

This was too much. "Again I flung him away from me, and again he returned. I think we could have played this game indefinitely." Kauffeld's solution, in the end, was to catch the annoying snake and stow it in a bag.

Saddled forever with the misnomer *constrictor* (due to a mix-up more than two hundred years ago when it was confused with the pilot rat snake, a *real* constrictor), the black racer is not a constrictor—it's a biter.

In fact, this snake has a genuinely rotten disposition, something I wish I had known when photographer John Netherton and I accompanied biologist Brian Miller on a field trip in Tennessee with his enthusiastic class of herpetology students. As John was preparing to photograph a juvenile black racer freshly caught by one of the students, he instructed me to prevent the snake from escaping. So I stuck out my hands—and was promptly bitten.

This presented something of a dilemma. I had no desire to be bitten again, even if this snake was only a juvenile, but I couldn't flinch either, since I had been introduced as the author of a forthcoming book about snakes and was, at that very moment, in the company of some pretty fearless snake hunters. Just then, Brian sauntered over to view the proceedings and casually pointed out that the snake's eyes were milky. Obviously, it was getting ready to shed.

Of course! That was why the little fel-

Juvenile black racer
Adult black racers are bold, demon-tempered serpents with jet black scales and a beautiful smooth finish. The equally testy juveniles are patterned with gray or chestnut brown blotches and are easily mistaken for juvenile black or gray rat snakes.

The black racer is not a true constrictor—it's actually a biter.

> Racers are cannibals and eat the young of their own species.

low kept assailing me: snakes with cloudy eyes often strike out wildly when harassed, due to their obstructed eyesight. To my own surprise, I began to feel sorry for the partially blinded racer, and I moved back into position to stoically endure more bites. Only later, when my research turned up numerous accounts by seasoned veterans who had been "viciously" attacked by "irate," "extremely irascible," and "quick-tempered" racers, did I recognize my folly.

Still, there's no denying that these slender, smooth-scaled snakes are strikingly beautiful. Both the Northern and Southern subspecies are jet black, with a milky white chin and throat and a whitish, gray, or yellow underside; juveniles are gray with reddish brown blotches or saddles. In the West, racers are usually tan, brown, bluish, or olive green. Racers' scales often appear glossy or satiny, and naturalist Thomas Tyning says they "seem to shine in the sunlight" and reveal a "lovely iridescence" in the right light.

Racers have large eyes and unusually good eyesight; the Northern subspecies has a prominent brown iris, and Southern racers have an even more striking red or orange iris. These long snakes (the record is 73 inches, or 1.85 m) often glide with their head raised off the ground and, if startled, demonstrate the accuracy of their name.

"I know of no snakes that are faster," writes Ditmars. "In an open field where a man can run," he claims, the racer "will lead the pursuer on a lively chase." On level ground, the man may win the race, but on a downward slope, the snake can beat the man.

Racers are active primarily by day, when they are more likely to encounter humans, and during the spring mating season they may advance on an intruder instead of flee-ing. If taken by surprise, a racer will sometimes vibrate its tail (as will many other nonvenomous species), the sound of which warns some interlopers and curdles the blood of others.

Open, dry habitats such as meadows, shrub grasslands, agricultural areas, and woodlands, as well as swampy margins of lakes, are favored by racers, which apparently have home territories. Recent studies with radio transmitters suggest that some racers return to specific retreats at night to sleep. Widely distributed throughout North America, racers can be found from the Atlantic to the Pacific coasts and from southern Canada to Mexico.

With wide-ranging tastes and a nondiscriminating appetite, these serpents feed on butterfly larvae, june bugs, cicadas, spiders, frogs, toads, lizards, snakes, mice, moles, rats, flying squirrels, and young birds. They are also cannibals and eat the young of their own species (and, occasionally, their own shed skins). Racers seize prey in their mouth or pin it to the ground with loops of the body before swallowing it.

Females lay clutches of two to thirty-one tough, leathery eggs, which are covered with coarse nodules of calcium resembling grains of salt. Many return year after year to communal nesting sites, generally located beneath flat stones or in rotten logs, rodent tunnels, mulch, or piles of sawdust.

Eastern Hog-Nosed Snake
Heterodon platirhinos

Two hundred years ago, word traveled back to Europe from America that a pugnacious variety of "poisonous" serpent—similar to the already infamous rattlesnake—threatened visitors to these shores.

"Of the venomous serpents which infest this water [the Great Lakes], the hissing snake is the most remarkable," one settler reported in 1793. "It blows from its mouth, with great force, a subtile wind [which], if drawn in with the breath of the unwary traveler, will infallibly bring a decline, that in a few months must prove mortal."

The snake with the celebrated hiss was the Eastern hog-nosed (or hognose) snake, a remarkable serpent that probably has more names than any other North American snake—including hissing adder, spreading adder, spreadhead, chunkhead, puff head, snubby viper, deaf adder, hay-nose snake, prairie rooter, and buckwheat-nose snake. To naturalist John Muir, it was simply the "blow snake," a thick, burly serpent often mistaken for a rattlesnake or cobra because of its celebrated defense repertoire and spreading hood.

When startled or harassed, the snake may first attempt to escape, often by burrowing. (Its upturned snout, the source of the unflattering porcine name, is ideal for this purpose.) But if an intruder is persistent, the hog-nosed snake will commence its time-honored routine.

"To see their act, you should behave as follows," Carr instructs. First, "make sure it is indeed a hog-nosed snake . . . and not a ground rattler." Next, move up to the snake and "sit down on the ground in front of him. He will coil, rear back . . . and lunge out at you repeatedly, each time hissing with almost intolerable menace." Steel yourself, Carr continues, and "reach over and pat the snake on the back."

Then witness a remarkable change.

After writhing in agony, the menacing snake will suddenly "wilt before your eyes, and he will proceed to prove that you have killed him." Rolling over onto his back, the snake will twist his head, open his mouth, and droop his tongue into the dirt, "as clearly defunct as any snake could be." But if you remain motionless and give the bluffer a few minutes, he will, in due course, raise his head and check your whereabouts. Flip him back onto his belly, and he will promptly roll over again, "thoroughly convinced," biologist W. J. Breckenridge explains, "that a dead snake should lie on its back."

Humans have long marveled at this snake's bravado and incomparable grasp of theatrics, while noting other defense maneuvers as well. The Eastern species, for example, often inflates its neck cobralike, up to three times its normal width (a habit less well developed in the Western species); it may also "strike" at its tormentor, although it keeps its mouth clamped shut, resulting in a bump rather than a bite. While contorting its body and writhing, the snake sometimes gapes its mouth wide, displaying a garish purple interior, and secretes an evil-smelling musk. If the ferocity of the loud hisses (audible at some distance), hood display, feints, and malodorous musk fail to discourage an intruder, the snake's sudden "death" might encourage a predator to leave the lifeless reptile for a period of time, returning to eat it later.

Some herpetologists, however, find it hard to believe that a predator would abandon a "freshly deceased morsel," and Steve Grenard argues that the hog-nosed snake's behavior is "undoubtedly genetically designed and chemically mediated," perhaps an epileptic seizure.

While the snake's upturned snout sometimes evokes snickers, the rostral scale is indispensable when burrowing. All three species—Eastern, Western, and Southern hog-nosed snakes—are found in sandy or otherwise relatively dry habitats, where

The Eastern hog-nosed snake has more names than any other North American snake: hissing adder, spreading adder, spreadhead, chunkhead, puff head, snubby viper, deaf adder, hay-nose snake, prairie rooter, and buckwheat-nose snake.

Eastern hog-nosed snake

Left, top: *The defensive behavior of the hog-nosed snake offers good theatre. When harassed, this snake will bluff shamelessly, sucking in air, hissing loudly, lunging with its head flattened, and spreading the skin of its neck like a cobra.*

Eastern hog-nosed snake

Left, bottom: *If its menacing display fails to scare off an intruder, a hog-nosed snake will writhe in agony, roll onto its back, extend its limp tongue, and feign death. Yet, if righted, it will quickly roll over again, "reasoning that a snake, to look thoroughly dead, should be lying on its back," herpetologist Raymond Ditmars once quipped.*

they plow into the soft earth to escape the midday sun or cold nighttime temperatures and to root out toads and other prey.

For years, scientists believed this snake's enlarged rear teeth were used to deflate toads, puncturing their skin and lungs when the amphibians puffed up to make themselves difficult to consume. Researchers now believe, however, that the snake channels mildly toxic venom into the bite; the ensuing envenomation "relaxes the toad for ease of swallowing," Ernst and Zug report. While humans apparently have little to fear from the snake's saliva, several cases of accidental envenomation have been recorded.

Individual snakes vary considerably in their ground coloring, from brown or gray to yellow, orange, or red, with irregular patterns or blotches of dark brown or black. The Eastern species is the largest of the three, reaching a record 45½ inches (1.16 m), but the average specimen is 20 to 33 inches (51 to 84 cm).

Worm Snake
Carphophis amoenus

Once, on a field trip to a Tennessee cedar glade, a young herpetology student asked me whether I would be interested in catching a worm snake.

"Are you kidding?" I responded scornfully. "I don't even want to *read* about worm snakes. Find something more *interesting*!"

But, as luck would have it, the youthful snake hunter did catch a worm snake, and, despite my obvious disdain, she handed it to me to examine. It was small, all right, but at least it had visible eyes (I had confused worm snakes with blind snakes). It immediately treated my fingers like a maze, probing every cleft with its tiny head in search of a way out.

At less than 6 inches (15.2 cm)—it's hard to measure a wiggling snake—this Eastern worm snake was not yet full-grown. Because my fingers were less satisfying than the moist earth beneath the limestone where it had been discovered, it continued to twist and turn, poking its head into every possible avenue of escape. Next it began coiling up, until it had spiraled its entire body around my index finger. Then it calmed down and began to size me up.

That was when I conceded that worm snakes are pretty interesting after all.

Generally plain brown or dark chestnut on their back, these snakes have a salmon or coral pink underside reminiscent of the ventral hues of a red-bellied or Southern ring-necked snake. (An all-pink female once turned up in Virginia.) The skin of all three subspecies—Eastern, Midwest, and Western—is smooth and glossy, sometimes characterized as "opalescent" because it reflects iridescent light.

Eastern worm snakes, also known as cricket or thunder snakes, range from Massachusetts down into Georgia and west to central Alabama; Midwest worm snakes are found east of the Mississippi River from southern Illinois and Ohio to the Gulf of Mexico; and the Western subspecies is found west of the Mississippi from Nebraska to northern Louisiana.

Worm snakes are shy and secretive, more often seen in April than in later months when summer heat builds and the ground dries up. During hot weather, worm snakes have been known to estivate at depths of 6 feet (1.8 m) or more. They are generally found in wooded areas, meadows, or agricultural areas, usually under stones, limestone rock, bark, decaying logs, or exposed leaf litter. Partial to moist earth, they are rarely seen in open areas unless their subterranean passages have become saturated or flooded. Their preference for moist locations leads them to turn up in suburban gardens and compost heaps.

Worm snakes average just 7½ to 11 inches (19 to 28 cm) in length.

Worm snake
Worm snakes are small, secretive creatures, generally found under rotting logs, decaying leaves, and stones. Averaging less than 10 inches (25 cm), a full-grown North American worm snake can be compared in size to a Polyphemus moth.

Blueberry farmers welcome red-bellied snakes, since they thrive on slugs that can damage fruit.

Diet is a factor in selecting an appropriate habitat, too, and, as their name might suggest, they do eat worms. But, more importantly, they also look like worms. While Western worm snakes have reached a record length of 15⅜ inches (39.1 cm)—pretty long for an earthworm—most worm snakes average just 7½ to 11 inches (19 to 28 cm).

In addition to their trademark cylindrical body, smooth scales, narrow head, and small eyes, worm snakes also boast an unusual physical feature (which they share with blind snakes): a sharp, spinelike tail. Although the function of this spine, according to Alan Tennant, is presumably to help the snake "gain purchase for pushing ahead through the constricted earthen matrix" (herpetologist Brian Miller refers to this maneuver as "thrust-creeping"), the point can also be used defensively.

"The worm snake," Tennant says, "may suddenly press its sharply pointed tail against a tender part of its captor's hand, producing a startling sensation so much like the prick of a tooth that one's invariable reflexive response is to drop the animal instantly."

These little snakes also exude a most unpleasant yellowish musk when harassed. It may not be as copious as the secretion from a garter snake, but worm snakes wriggle so much when held that they do a masterful job of smearing it on their captor, whether it's a human, skunk, mole, owl, cat, or another snake.

The reproductive habits of worm snakes are poorly understood, though scientists believe females can store the male's sperm over the winter if necessary. Generally, a clutch consists of two to eight eggs the size of drugstore cold capsules, deposited under rocks or in decaying logs or under-

ground burrows.

Humans pose a very real threat to worm snake populations today. Ernst and Barbour worry that the snake's habitat is becoming increasingly fragmented as large tracts of land are converted to urban and suburban use; furthermore, indiscriminate use of pesticides causes the death of worm snakes that eat poisoned insects.

Red-Bellied Snake
Storeria occipitomaculata

The red-bellied snake is the Walter Mitty of North American serpents. Like the shy, retiring, and inoffensive husband in James Thurber's short story "The Secret Life of Walter Mitty," this small snake is "as innocuous a snake as exists anywhere," herpetologist W. J. Breckenridge declares.

That probably explains why red-bellied snakes aren't considered charismatic or glamorous and are seldom displayed in reptile collections. Their size doesn't help, either: like earth snakes and worm snakes (which this species resembles in several ways), red-bellied snakes are quite short, with adults averaging just 8 to 10 inches (20.3 to 25.4 cm) and achieving a record length of only 16 inches (40.6 cm).

Yet anyone who has kept a red-belly for any period of time has probably succumbed to this snake's subtle charms—and perhaps discovered that, like Walter Mitty, the red-belly has a flip side, literally and figuratively.

Seen from above, the red-bellied snake looks rather nondescript, ranging in color from light or dark brown to slate gray or black (sometimes with one or more darker stripes) and sporting a light ring formed by three small spots on the neck. The underside, however, is generally brilliant red or vermilion, or occasionally a light orange or yellow. Since the young of this nocturnal species are usually jet black with a whitish ring and pinkish belly, they are easily mistaken for juvenile ring-necked snakes. When harassed, this snake is quick to display its bright belly and emit a particularly strong musk, and some individuals roll onto their backs and play dead when alarmed.

Joseph Mitchell and others insist this snake "will not bite" (its mouth is too small to inflict injury), but Breckenridge says that its tiny teeth can "cling to the epidermis of its captor's finger." Some red-bellies have a peculiar habit of curling their upper lip when first handled, exposing the black lining of their mouth. This odd behavior, which Albert and Anna Wright call a "facial defense," displays the teeth of the upper jaw in such a way that, to humans, it looks like the snake is grinning.

Red-bellied snakes are commonly found in woodlands and near sphagnum bogs, but they seem to turn up in a wide variety of habitats, especially under rocks, logs,

Northern red-bellied snake
Right, top: *Viewed from underneath, the celebrated red abdomen of a Northern red-bellied snake—occasionally orange or pale yellow in adults and pinkish in juveniles—becomes visible. Though these small snakes are inconspicuous and inoffensive, they have a curious habit of curling their upper lip when harassed, exposing their teeth and pricking a handler's skin.*

Northern red-bellied snake
Right, bottom: *Red-bellied snakes are secretive woodland dwellers whose small size and nocturnal foraging behavior keep them out of the public eye. An anthill in Manitoba once yielded 101 red-bellies hibernating alongside more than 150 green snakes and garter snakes.*

There are at least thirteen subspecies of ring-necked snakes, ranging in color from slate gray to blue gray, black to olive green.

woodpiles, debris, and leaf mold, or in the vicinity of abandoned barns, houses, and automobiles. Occasionally, they are sighted swimming close to shore or climbing low shrubs and poison ivy. Because these snakes hunt for prey in small cracks and chinks, they also turn up in basements and window wells.

Red-bellied snakes range from southern Canada southward through Minnesota to Texas and eastward to central Florida, with scattered populations in the Black Hills of South Dakota. Their principal diet consists of slugs, snails, and earthworms, along with various insects, millipedes, and larvae. (Blueberry farmers welcome red-bellied snakes, since they thrive on slugs that can damage fruit.) In captivity, these snakes become tame enough to feed right out of a human hand. Despite their obvious shyness and propensity to hide, some exhibit an endearing sense of curiosity, lifting their heads out of leaf debris or moss to observe nearby movement or activity.

In the wild, these snakes have been discovered in large aggregations, perhaps to reduce moisture loss during overwintering. (In 1934 a Canadian farmer found 101 red-bellies sharing their quarters with 148 green snakes and 8 plains garter snakes.) Mating occurs during spring as well as summer and fall, and females give birth to live young in broods of one to twenty-one. A female found in Manitoba possessed a copulatory plug similar to those detected in female red-sided garter snakes.

Ring-Necked Snake
Diadophis punctatus

The first time I encountered a ring-necked snake in the Deep South I was caught off guard. Up North, this curious little serpent has a distinctive yellow ring around its neck and a rather unmemorable yellow or cream-colored underside; in the South, however, a portion of the snake's belly is scarlet—easily confused with that of a red-bellied snake.

But that's not all. Some Southern and Western populations *behave* differently, too. When threatened, these subspecies rear their tail, flashing the vividly colored underside, and coil into a spiral that looks remarkably like a corkscrew. (This bizarre pose accounts for several nicknames, including corkscrew snake and thimble snake.) The scarlet underside may be flashed to startle a predator, and the tail coil may intimidate an enemy or divert attention from the more vulnerable head. Alternatively, the bright color could be a warning signal, like the fiery crimson of a dart-poison frog or the bright bands of a coral snake, as scientists now suspect the saliva of ring-necked snakes harbors a mild venom (not a threat to humans).

Typically these snakes, of which there are at least thirteen subspecies, have a somber slate gray, blue gray, black, brown, or olive body color. In some populations, half-moon-shaped spots appear in a single row down the bright red or orange abdomen. The snake's iris is black, with a blood-red ring around the pupil. While the multiplicity of subspecies range from coast to coast and from southern Canada to northern Mexico, their distribution is spotty in dry regions of the West.

Ring-necked snakes are small and slender, averaging just 8 to 15 inches (20 to 38 cm), though they are sometimes longer in the West. While field researchers regard the species as "sociable" (aggregations of up to ten are sometimes found under rocks or rotting logs), it is also highly reclusive. Henry Fitch, who studied a Kansas ring-

necked population for twenty-seven years, characterized this snake as "difficult to observe" under natural conditions.

Most favor moist soil conditions and will estivate underground if a summer is unusually hot or dry. Woodlands are the favored habitats, but grassy shrublands, pastures, limestone hilltops, and prairies near water are also popular. In the San Francisco Bay area, Robert Stebbins reports, ring-necks sometimes turn up in salt marshes. Usually discovered beneath leaf litter, fallen bark, or flat stones, ring-necked snakes also turn up surprisingly often in suburban gardens, where they are attracted by earthworms. Glimpsed primarily at night, they also eat salamanders, frogs, lizards, slugs, grubs, and small insects. Vertebrate prey may be constricted.

Despite small mouths, these snakes have relatively large posterior teeth that can inject mildly venomous saliva into their prey, which is gripped or chewed before swallowing. (Conant and Collins report that drops

Ring-necked snake

Sporting a distinctive gold-yellow collar and a yellow or reddish belly, the secretive ring-necked snake is usually found in moist leaf litter or under logs and rocks. Some ring-necks will twist their tail into a tight corkscrew and display their colorful underside, perhaps to startle a predator or divert attention from their more vulnerable head.

of saliva sometimes appear at the corner of the mouth when a specimen is held.) When molested, these harmless snakes will squirm vigorously, lashing their tails from side to side and secreting a smelly musk; others assume the corkscrew position or play dead.

During the summer, females deposit two to ten eggs in damp soil beneath flat rocks or in rotting logs, frequently alongside eggs of their own or other species. The long white eggs have thin, leathery shells and are curved like a boomerang.

Corn Snake
Elaphe guttata

There are two perfectly good explanations why this North American serpent is called a corn snake: first, because it is frequently found in cornfields and corn cribs, searching for rodents attracted by the ripening kernels; and second, because the rich colors and patterned underside bring to mind the checkered appearance of Indian corn.

No matter which explanation pertains, the corn snake, or red rat snake, is one of America's most beautiful nonvenomous snakes. Colored in warm browns, oranges, and yellows, with crimson or chestnut blotches and saddles outlined in black, it looks like "a milk snake that has been dyed scarlet," says Percy Morris. The white abdomen is heavily checkered or marbled with black. Starting behind the head, a wedge-shaped spearpoint marking extends to between the eyes. (Because of their similarity in colors and patterns, corn snakes are frequently mistaken for copperheads and killed.)

With such a handsome appearance, it's no wonder that corn snakes are popular pets in the United States and Europe, where a wide variety of color morphs are bred and sold. "If this genetic monkey-business continues," complain Ray Staszko and Jerry Walls, "one day soon attempting to describe a typical corn snake will be like trying to describe the color of a typical house cat."

Corn snakes range from the pine barrens of New Jersey southward to Key West and west to the Mississippi River, with disjunct populations in Nebraska, Colorado, and Utah. Partial to sandy pine and oak woods, rocky hillsides, the edges of streams, and abandoned buildings and barns, corn snakes sometimes turn up in the basements of churches, hotels, and factories, along rail lines, near public swimming pools, and, according to Albert and Anna Wright, in storm sewers and abandoned pipelines.

Rarely seen abroad during the daytime, this secretive snake retreats by day to rodent burrows and underground tunnels created by tree roots or hides beneath sheltering objects or the loose bark of decaying stumps and logs; around sunset, it emerges to hunt mice, rats, and birds.

The apparent tameness of corn snakes in captivity misleads humans into presuming they are equally mild-mannered in the wild, but many snake collectors have learned that this snake has an unpredictable temperament. According to Ditmars, corn snakes are "bold and strong reptiles, showing considerable bravery when cornered and little of the rush and fluster of most snakes when taken unawares." Although inclined to glide to safety if permitted, a corn snake taken by surprise will coil and strike, hissing sharply and vibrating its tail.

Relatively stout and breadloaf-shaped in cross section, corn snakes grow 2 to 6 feet long (0.6 to 1.83 m). Their preferred diet

Corn snakes are frequently found in cornfields and corn cribs, searching for rodents attracted by the ripening kernels.

Corn snake
Above: *The corn snake of the Eastern and South-eastern United States is a common visitor to corn-fields, where it searches for mice and other rodents. These quick-tempered serpents will strike boldly when cornered, often vibrating their tail in dry leaves and scaring humans who mistake the sound for that of a rattlesnake.*

Okeetee corn snake
Left: *The Okeetee corn snake, a native of the Okeetee plantation area of Jasper County, South Carolina, is highly prized among collectors for its rich crimson or chestnut saddle-shaped blotches, edged in black and set against a background of orange, gray, or tan.*

"Behold the very paradise of snakes."
—Joseph Conrad, *Nostromo*, 1904

consists of mice, rats, moles, bats, birds, frogs, and lizards, which they kill by constriction before eating. Their reputation for effective rodent control is well deserved, and farmers consider them to be good neighbors. Females lay clutches of three to thirty eggs in communal nesting sites, which include damp sawdust piles, rotting timber, and animal burrows.

Yellow Rat Snake
Elaphe obsoleta quadrivittata

The yellow rat snake (or chicken snake, as it is sometimes known) is a "large, strong, and swift serpent," botanist William Bartram observed in 1791. "They are a domestic snake, haunting about houses and plantations, and would be useful to man if tamed and properly tutored, being great devourers of rats, but they are apt to disturb hen-roosts and prey upon chickens. They are as innocent as a worm with respect to venom, are easily tamed, and soon become very familiar."

Bartram had it right: yellow rat snakes are indeed valuable as rodent catchers, and if they could only be "properly tutored" to stay out of hen houses, they would be the farmer's perfect partner. When Ernst and Barbour taught at the University of Kentucky, local farmers would come to them every year to ask for "excess rat snakes," which the farmers released in their barns and corn cribs.

Many farmers, however, grow nervous when they see a chicken snake on the prowl. Although the snake is probably headed for the nearest chicken coop in search of rats and mice, it may succumb to the temptation of eggs or chicks instead. Years ago, when farmers placed stone or china "nest eggs" in chicken coops to induce fowl to lay eggs, they sometimes discovered these objects inside the stomachs of visiting rat snakes.

These serpents can cause other trouble, too. In Virginia, for example, black rat snakes have been known to "enter power transformers, become electrocuted, and cause power outages," Mitchell reports. One incident left 13,000 homes without power.

The yellow rat snake is one of five recognized subspecies of the rat snake in the United States (the other four are the black rat, gray rat, Everglades rat, and Texas rat snake). This particular race is strikingly handsome, with four dark stripes on a yellow, golden yellow, greenish yellow, or grayish ground color. Hatchlings are born with prominent spots or blotches.

Like other rat snakes, this subspecies is an expert climber, as likely to be spotted in the rafters of a stable or in the hollow of a live oak as in a farmer's field or a cypress swamp. Ditmars recalls a yellow rat snake that regularly sunned itself in a live oak some 25 feet (7.6 m) from the ground, and Carr kept one in his laboratory that would climb to the ceiling at the corner of the room "with no support other than the rough surface of the plaster." In cross section, this snake is shaped like a loaf of bread, Conant and Collins note, which helps the snake press its belly scales against irregularities in tree bark or other surfaces to obtain a grip.

The rat snake's penchant for climbing trees, where it seeks birds' eggs, hatchlings, tree frogs, and flying squirrels, occasionally ruffles the feathers of bird lovers, who bristle when they glimpse a yellow or gray rat snake peering out of the entrance to a red-cockaded woodpecker's nest cavity. To fend off high-climbing rat snakes, this endangered species has developed an inge-

The yellow rat snake is sometimes known as the chicken snake.

Yellow rat snake

Above: *The handsomely colored yellow rat snake of the American South spends much of its time in live oaks, cypress, and even rafters of barns, where it hunts for birds' nests and squirrels. Farmers often call rat snakes "chicken snakes" because of their appetite for poultry.*

Everglades rat snake

Right: *A bright orange or red resident of southern Florida, the Everglades rat snake is commonly glimpsed in sawgrass and roadside pine trees. Unlike other rat snakes, which have black tongues, this subspecies sports a distinctive red tongue.*

Milk snake

According to American folklore, milk snakes sneak into barns and suck milk from unsuspecting cows. These brown- or red-blotched constrictors actually enter stables and other buildings in search of mice and rats, which they consume in far greater numbers than do hawks and owls.

When handled by humans, milk snakes often become belligerent, hissing, striking, vibrating their tail, and spraying musk.

nious environmental barrier.

The red-cockaded woodpecker, ornithologist Jerome Jackson writes, excavates its nest in pine trees, where it makes small holes, or "resin wells," to create a "continuous flow of pine gum" around the cavity entrance and tree. In controlled field experiments, Jackson found that rat snakes would writhe in pain (or die) after climbing logs coated with this sticky resin, which not only impedes movement by cementing overlapping scales together but also contains acidic compounds highly toxic to snakes.

Over the years, the yellow rat snake has acquired a reputation for boldness and fearlessness, as it will quickly face an intruder with its mouth open and hiss loudly. The distinctive black tongue is visible when the snake lunges, and the tail vibrates rapidly. If handled, this snake will excrete an unpleasant-smelling creamy musk, which Floridians Pete Carmichael and Winston Williams say is highly enticing to wild and domestic cats.

Yellow rat snakes can grow quite long—the record is 7 feet 3 inches (2.21 m)—and average 42 to 72 inches (1.06 to 1.83 m) in length. Ranging from peninsular Florida northward along the Atlantic coast into North Carolina, they sometimes breed with other rat snakes and produce "intergrade" specimens. About two dozen hatchlings are born in August or September. In Florida, some rat snakes estivate during an especially hot summer; farther north, rat snakes hibernate during the winter, seeking out rocky crevices, stumps, logs, abandoned burrows, and old wells.

Years ago, while collecting reptiles in Georgia, Ditmars heard someone scream in a small cabin and saw a large aluminum pot fly out the window. "As it struck the ground," he later recalled, "a big coiled chicken snake rolled out." Checking with the occupants of the cabin, Ditmars learned from the mother that she had been peeling potatoes for her family and had reached up to a shelf for a cooking pot. "The pot felt heavy, and, poking inside, she discovered the snake neatly coiled within it." Ditmars savored the anecdote—and kept the snake.

Milk Snake
Lampropeltis triangulum

As more and more Americans leave their rural roots behind, the myth of the thirsty milk snake drinking from a dairy cow appears to have nearly run its course. Not many years ago, however, authors of books about snakes felt obligated to consign this particular piece of folklore to the manure heap (most appropriately, since it is a favored site for females to lay their eggs).

That the North American milk snake would have the cheek or physical dexterity to slip up on a cow and suck its milk, as the old wives' tale suggested, is sheer nonsense—"about as likely to happen as for witches to start flying over our heads on broomsticks," says Percy Morris. The milk snake "has little ability to suck fluids," Ernst and Barbour point out, "and besides, what cow would stand still for having its teats grasped by a mouth with so many sharp teeth!"

The origins of the milk snake's name remind us that this North American serpent was once common around cow barns and cellars where milk was kept, but other unusual names have been applied as well: red adder, chain snake, checkered snake, horn snake, sachem snake, thunder-and-lightning snake, house moccasin, and cowsucker. By whatever name, this serpent has "one of the largest ranges of any snake in the world," Conant and Collins report, with as many as twenty-five subspecies ranging from Canada all the way to Ecuador.

Although its average length is a moderate 2 to 3 feet (61 to 90 cm), the milk snake makes a lasting impression and is highly prized in the pet trade because of its striking colors and pattern: large rings, blotches, or saddles of red or chestnut brown, yellow, cream, and black. Considerable confusion is created by the milk snake's resemblance to other nonvenomous, and one venomous, species. Eastern milk snakes, for example, are sometimes confused with corn and fox snakes, while red, Louisiana, Central Plains, and Mexican milk snakes, among others, are confused with the scarlet kingsnake and the venomous coral snake. Milk snake intergrades complicate identification even further.

Yet despite their colorful markings, these secretive snakes are rarely seen by day, unless one probes their hiding places, which include stumps, fallen logs, rock piles, and debris in woodlands, hummocks, fields, sand dunes, or around dwellings where rodents are plentiful. Milk snakes rarely bask in direct sunlight, apparently preferring to remain beneath sun-warmed rocks, Collins explains, to maintain an "optimal" body temperature.

Milk snakes feed principally on small rodents, lizards, other snakes (including rattlesnakes, whose venom they may be largely immune to), frogs, and fish, but they will also climb considerable heights in search of birds' eggs. Breckenridge reports a milk snake was once spotted climbing the side of a house to reach a sparrow's nest in a tall rosebush.

When handled by humans, milk snakes often become belligerent, hissing, striking, vibrating their tail, and spraying musk. In captivity, when an individual is held, "it may leisurely swing its head to one side, grasp you somewhere in the vicinity of your wrist, and start chewing," Morris says. "There is no pretense of a sudden strike, as one would expect from a snake, just a slow, deliberate 'flank attack' that takes one by surprise." When the wrist is jerked away, the recurved teeth lacerate the skin and draw blood.

Milk snakes are egg layers, and females often converge on communal egg-laying sites in early summer to deposit their clutches of three to twenty eggs. Frequently, females will coil around their eggs until they hatch.

Gray-Banded Kingsnake
Lampropeltis alterna

In December 1901, a new species of North American kingsnake was formally described for the first time. Discovered in the Davis Mountains of western Texas, the new species was unusual because it lacked the prominent white or yellow rings commonly found on other kingsnakes; instead, there were crossbands of gunmetal gray and reddish orange, divided by thin black bands.

Dubbed the "Davis Mountain kingsnake," it was considered by some herpetologists just a subspecies of the Mexican kingsnake; as a result, its scientific name has been in flux ever since. Today, it is popularly known as the gray-banded kingsnake.

Strangely, by the early 1940s only five specimens had been found and described; in fact, Tennant says, the serpent came to be regarded as "among the rarest North American reptiles." More recently, however,

The scarcity of the gray-banded kingsnake is probably due to the near-impossibility of locating these reptiles within the limestone catacombs they inhabit beneath the earth's surface.

Gray-banded kingsnake

A secretive inhabitant of mountain ranges and rocky canyons in western Texas and northern Mexico, the gray-banded kingsnake is admired for its distinctive red-orange saddles on wide slate gray crossbands, edged with narrow black borders. Although some specimens are gentle, others thrash about and secrete an offensive odor when handled.

herpetologists have had reason to revise their thinking.

The "notorious scarcity" of this snake, Tennant explains, is probably due less to a limited population than to "the near-impossibility of locating these reptiles within the limestone catacombs they inhabit beneath the surface." In other words, this snake may not be rare—just rarely seen. (This proved an important distinction for the federal government, which denied the snake federal protection as a threatened species in 1980.)

Contributing to the confusion was the discovery in 1950 of a different color morph—the "Blair's phase"—which has fewer than fifteen orange-red saddles, compared to the "*alterna* phase," which sports up to twenty-three saddles and has thin black bands between the saddles. Yet another phase, the variable or Thayer's kingsnake, produces "milk-snake forms, gray-banded kingsnake forms, and even melanistic forms . . . sometimes within the same clutch of eggs," according to Gerold and Cindy Merker.

Some observers believe the snake's vivid orange-red bands make it especially vulnerable to predators, while others insist a subterranean lifestyle precludes the need for camouflage. Tennant says that at night their nonreflective back closely resembles twisted creosote branches.

Due to its striking, if variable, appearance, this snake is one of the "most desirable" serpents for collectors, Tennant reports, and he recalls a period when dozens of cars could be seen cruising on roads through the mountains from dusk till dawn, hunting for these snakes. (An early-evening thunderstorm would usually enhance the hunters' prospects.)

The gray-banded kingsnake has large, protruding eyes with round black pupils on a pale gray iris. The belly, also pale gray, is usually bedecked with irregular black blotches, which sometimes blend together. Because this snake has a somewhat triangular-shaped head, with a pointed snout and slender neck, it is occasionally mistaken for a rattlesnake.

These moderate-sized snakes average 20 to 36 inches (51 to 90 cm), although the record is 57¾ inches (1.47 m). Their preferred habitats include rocky limestone hillsides, canyons, mountains, and desert flats, where sotol cactus and acacia trees dominate. The crumbly limestone flags and substrate of their range in Mexico's Chihuahuan Desert and the Trans-Pecos region of western Texas and northern Mexico are pocketed with so many airholes and hidden passageways that scientists believe gray-banded kingsnakes could spend virtually their entire lives there, unseen by visitors and thriving on local populations of lizards and pocket mice cornered in their subterranean retreats.

Garter Snakes
Thamnophis

"And so we went for the snakes, and grabbed a couple of dozen garters," Huck Finn relates in *The Adventures of Huckleberry Finn*, "and put them in a bag, and put it in our room, and by that time it was suppertime. . . . And there warn't a blessed snake up there when we went back—we didn't half tie the sack, and they worked out somehow, and left. But it didn't matter much, because they was still on the premises somewheres. . . .

"You'd see them dripping from the rafters and places every now and then; and they generly landed in your plate, or down the back of your neck, and most of the time where you didn't want them. Well, they was handsome and striped, and there warn't no harm in a million of them; but that never made no difference to Aunt Sally. . . . Every time one of them flopped down on her, it

Thayer's kingsnake
Thayer's kingsnake, a subspecies of the Mexican kingsnake, occurs in a variety of gray-banded or milk snake color morphs, sometimes within the same clutch of eggs. Difficult to identify, these snakes are also hard to find, taking shelter in passageways beneath limestone floors of desert flats and foothills.

Garter snakes are also known as garden snakes, grass snakes, and striped snakes.

didn't make no difference what she was doing, she would just lay that work down and light out. And you could hear her whoop to Jericho."

Garter snakes really do have a knack for surprising folks, and Mark Twain couldn't resist sneaking this episode into his novel because, as a boy, he'd pulled the same stunt.

From Twain's beloved South to the Northwest Territories of Canada, garter snakes are the most geographically widespread and ecologically successful snakes in North America. Their range includes every state in the continental United States and extends "much farther northward than any other snake in the Western Hemisphere," report Douglas Rossman, Neil Ford, and Richard Seigel. By the mid-1990s, these herpetologists had counted thirty different species, one of which, the common garter snake, has at least eleven recognized subspecies.

Yet many people don't appreciate garter snakes, and for good reason: they bite. (When I worked as a nature counselor at a Wisconsin summer camp, I was bitten and smeared with musk so many times that I uncharitably renounced the whole lot of them as vengeful and wicked.)

The Eastern and Chicago garter snakes of my youth went by several names, including garden snake, grass snake, and striped snake. Some, I realize now, were probably their look-alike relatives the ribbon snakes. Nonetheless, of all the snakes in the Upper Midwest, this was the one nearly everyone recognized. They were fast moving, usually grew no more than about 2 feet (60 cm) long, and were streaked with yellow stripes on a green or brown (or black, olive, or bluish) background. And each one had a mouth that seemed to be grinning at you.

Garter snakes owe their name to their resemblance to the stripes on men's old-

Checkered garter snake
The checkered garter snake sports a bold checkerboard pattern, which makes it an easy target on roads, where it is known to scavenge for toads. During World War II, this common backyard resident was crowned the "king of the victory gardens" in Texas.

fashioned garter straps. One subspecies, the San Francisco garter snake, appears on the list of federally endangered species and is considered to be America's rarest (and perhaps most beautiful) snake; graced with handsome red stripes, cinnamon-colored eyes, and a turquoise belly, it was featured on a U.S. postage stamp in 1996.

Because their range is so expansive and their habitats so varied, this genus may be the best-studied in the world. As a result, the red-sided garter snake, a native of the Great Plains and western Canada, has come to share many salient details of its spectacular sex life with curious tourists and inquisitive scientists.

Herpetologist Robert Mason, who has been studying this species for more than sixteen years, calls the annual phenomenon of "snake balls," which can be observed when the serpents emerge from hibernation at their Manitoba den complexes, a "fantastic" sight, with "tens of thousands of snakes just milling around in big knots." The males, which appear first, swarm over the females in lopsided ratios of ten to one hundred males per female. "Fittingly, it is a tradition in southern Manitoba for tourists to come see these mating displays on Mother's Day," note Rossman et al., "which coincides with the peak of the courtship rituals."

As if these remarkable breeding frenzies weren't enough ("imagine bowls of lively, amorous reptilian spaghetti," says writer Michael Lipske), the red-sided garter snake is famous for two other quirks: the copulatory plug and the "she-male" masquerade.

When males emerge from hibernation at the Manitoba dens, they must actively compete for a mate against thousands of rivals. Some males have evolved a clever strategy to obtain a competitive edge: they secrete a chemical that serves as a copulatory plug in the oviductal openings of the female's cloaca immediately after copulating. This plug makes the female "temporarily unavailable to other males," explains Michael Devine, and it "reduces the likelihood of multiple inseminations."

The other male strategy is to mimic a female by means of chemicals. For this ruse, some males release female-specific pheromones—apparently indistinguishable from female pheromones—that attract other males. The advantage to the "she-male," conclude Robert Mason and David Crews, "lies in an ability to gain a better position in the mating ball by confusing other males."

Although it was once believed that garter snakes mate only in the spring, researchers have observed fall matings and now recognize that mating cycles vary. Females give birth to relatively large broods of live young, with litters ranging from three to as many as eighty offspring or more.

Garter snakes are foragers, actively following chemical trails left by frogs, toads, worms, salamanders, and leeches. They are often found near water and, when foraging for fish, can be seen swimming with their mouths open.

The tendency of garter snakes to strike at their persecutors and hold onto their prey has led biologists to hypothesize that enzymes in garter snake saliva may immobilize their prey. The teeth of these snakes can cause profuse bleeding in humans, and the Duvernoy's gland identified in several specimens may explain cases of human envenomation.

Many garter snakes are characterized as wanderers, which is how a Western subspe-

Garter snakes owe their name to their resemblance to the stripes on men's old-fashioned garter straps.

97

Water snakes hibernate during the winter in the North, usually in mud at the bottom of a body of water, although some have been found in muskrat dens and beaver lodges.

cies called the wandering garter snake acquired its name. Garter snakes implanted with radio transmitters have traveled surprisingly long distances between their summer feeding ranges and hibernation dens (in Manitoba, the annual exodus takes them directly through suburban yards), and scientists believe that solar cues play a role in their orientation and navigation.

Time and again, garter snakes have demonstrated an extraordinary tolerance for cold temperatures, and they are often the first to emerge in the spring and the last to hibernate in the fall. While many aggregate in deep underground dens, others seek out animal burrows, logs, stumps, or rocks. Eastern garter snakes discovered hibernating in abandoned farm wells in the North can survive in cold waters beneath surface-level ice. Scientists conducting a research experiment once found a number of garters accidentally entombed in ice after a motor had failed. They immediately began thawing their frozen subjects—slowly—and the snakes soon recovered from their ordeal.

While many garter snakes find humans a major annoyance and source of grief, the reverse is true too: after Steven Spielberg's movie character Indiana Jones fell into a traincar full of garter snakes as a boy, he was traumatized for life.

Water Snakes
Nerodia

Once, while boating on the Savannah River, Ditmars heard a wild thrashing in the nearby brush and a great crash that startled other members of his party. His guide, an experienced woodsman, declared that "nothing but a bear could make so much noise" and fired two rounds of buckshot into the center of the disturbance.

Hearing no further commotion, the group moved on.

Later than day, upon their return, the herpetologist noticed a huge brown water snake stretched out on the sagging brush; when approached, it threw itself down and "thrashed violently from side to side, producing a noise like the progress of a cow through the bushes."

As blusterous as a bear and as clamorous as a cow, the North American water snake is a remarkable reptile, though often in a vexsome way. Anyone who has ever been bitten by a water snake is not likely to forget the experience. One herpetologist characterizes these snakes as "quite nippy"; others use such descriptions as "vicious," "sinister when cornered," and "extraordinarily disagreeable."

Scientists currently recognize nine species of North American water snakes, most of them concentrated in the South; the Northern water snake, however, ranges from Maine west to Colorado, and the plainbelly, diamondback, and several other species can be found from Texas northward into the Mississippi Valley. In southern Florida, swarms of water snakes could once be seen on the Tamiami Trail, and Kauffeld recalls an old saying that "an automobile could skid from Tampa to Miami on their crushed bodies." These semi-aquatic serpents are found on the borders of lakes, ponds, streams, and rivers and take up residence in "virtually every swamp, marsh, or bog" within their range, Conant and Collins report.

Water snakes are relatively large, with stout bodies and wide heads. The record length for a Northern water snake is 4 feet 7⅛ inches (140.5 cm), while the diamondback water snake has reached a whopping 5 feet 3 inches (160 cm). Ditmars charac-

Albino water snake
North American water snakes are nervous and ill-tempered, thrashing about and striking viciously when disturbed. Albino specimens, such as this individual found at Reelfoot Lake in west Tennessee, rarely survive long in the wild because they are so conspicuous.

terizes water snakes as "ugly," and Morris calls them "as vicious-looking as the most venomous snake that ever lived." Many species are dark brown or gray, with black or reddish brown markings; as individuals age, their colors tend to fade or darken, making their patterns more obscure.

Henry David Thoreau, describing a large, drab water snake in his journal in 1858, noted that the snake looked "uniformly dark brown" while sunning on a bank, "but, in the water, broad reddish-brown bars are seen, very distinctly, alternating with very dark brown ones."

Since their colors and markings resemble those of the notorious cottonmouth, it is important to note that water snakes have round pupils, whereas cottonmouths have elliptical pupils; in addition, the cottonmouth has a pair of pits on the forward part of its head, near the nostrils, and the interior of its mouth is white. Water snakes tend to move more quickly than cottonmouths and do not vibrate their tails when aroused as cottonmouths do.

The collector who can outrace a water snake and grab it before it plunges into the water not only has to deal with a very muscular snake, but also with sharp teeth and copious musk glands. A few benevolent herpetologists claim that bites by water snakes are no worse than minor scratches, but most comment on their disagreeable nature and inclination to bite. When naturalist Edward O. Wilson caught green water snakes as a youth, their sharp teeth made his blood run freely. Now scientists know why: the saliva of some contains an anticoagulant. To complicate matters, several species have slightly toxic secretions, which are effective against their natural prey.

Frogs rank high on the water snake's list

of diet preferences, and "if you go to see why a frog is screaming," Carr declares, "you will probably find a water snake." Other prey include salamanders, crustaceans, insects, small mammals, and birds. Northern water snakes have been known to herd tadpoles and small fish toward the bank of a pond, then loop around them before consuming them. In captivity, water snakes will learn to eat canned sardines and chopped fish, and when the scent of fish or frog is smeared across the bottom of a cage, these snakes will dart about wildly and bite one another in their frenzy to locate the missing prey.

Water snakes hibernate during the winter in the North, usually in mud at the bottom of a body of water, although individuals have been discovered in muskrat dens and beaver lodges; others migrate upland, where they seek out underground chambers. Temperatures in much of the South, on the other hand, allow water snakes to remain active year round. In the spring, water snakes sometimes congregate in large numbers, making it easier for males to find a mate. Females, which are generally larger and heavier, give birth to live young, often in litters as large as sixty or more.

Mud Snake
Farancia abacura

Big Muddy. To some folks that means the Mississippi River, but to a snake collector it could be a large specimen of mud snake, a.k.a. the stinger snake, horn snake, dart snake, hook snake, hoop snake, thunder snake, wampum snake, barrel hooper, or stingaree.

The mud snake may be snubbed because its common name sounds drab and lacks flash, but it deserves better. That's because

Mud snake
Mud snakes have glossy, ebony black iridescent scales and bright "flash colors" of reddish or pink on the underside. This specimen's eyes are nearly opaque, indicating it is about to shed its skin.

Mud snakes are also known as hoop snakes, stingarees, and dart snakes.

Mud snakes' tails have a hardened, needlelike scale or spine at the tip that is sharp enough to prick a finger and draw blood.

this snake, even though it inhabits the muddy bottoms of waterways, marshes, and swamps, is anything but muddy in appearance. Iridescent purple to ebony black on its upper half, the mud snake is vivid red, vermilion, or salmon pink underneath, with black blotches or bars. The overall effect is glossy and enamel-like, with a glistening, metallic sheen and smooth scales.

When resting, a mud snake sometimes forms a large loop, which has fooled even an expert like Ditmars into mistaking this snake for a discarded bicycle tire. While that accounts for the name "hoop snake," the names "stingaree" and "dart snake" refer to the tail, which has a hardened, needlelike scale or spine at the tip—sharp enough to prick a finger and draw blood.

Human targets aside, the spiny tip of the tail is useful for manipulating tadpoles, frogs, fish, and eel-like amphibians such as amphiumas and greater sirens into position for swallowing. Furthermore, the sharp tip is often employed during a tussle to puncture the soft, scaleless bodies of these slippery aquatic creatures. Some mud snakes are so partial to amphiumas and sirens that specimens in captivity may starve themselves to death rather than eat anything else.

Another significant adaptation for preying on these amphibians is a set of enlarged teeth at the rear of the snake's upper jaw, which help to hold slippery food. Discovery of a Duvernoy's gland in one specimen has generated speculation that, like rear-fanged snakes, these snakes may inject a mild toxin to subdue their prey. Despite its unusually large rear teeth and menacing tail spine, the mud snake is quite docile and

"will not bite" humans, Carmichael and Williams maintain. In fact, Albert and Anna Wright say their children exhibited a genuine "fondness" for mud snakes and begged to have their photos taken with a mud snake draped across their necks. One child even played with the snake "as a doll, put it in a corner of the couch, covered it up and seemed to take satisfaction in knowing it was quiet there. The snake made no effort to get away."

The two subspecies of mud snake—Eastern and Western—inhabit the southern United States, the former ranging from southern Virginia to Florida, the latter from Alabama to eastern Texas and northward into southern Illinois. Eastern mud snakes average 40 to 54 inches (1.02 to 1.37 m) and attain a record of 84 inches (2.13 m), while the Western subspecies averages 30 to 48 inches (0.76 to 1.21 m).

Mud snakes burrow avidly into mud, clay, and other soft soils, and all are excellent swimmers, occasionally entering salt marshes and other brackish waters. In the fall, they leave the water and burrow into decaying pine stumps or soil to overwinter. An anthropologist excavating Indian mounds in Florida once came across some mud snakes that had burrowed 10 feet (3.05 m) into a sandy bank.

Females sometimes coil around their egg clutches during incubation in nests dug in sandy soil, heaps of dead hyacinths, or even alligator nests. In 1929 a mud snake killed on a Florida highway was found carrying 104 eggs, making this species one of the world's most fertile snakes; other specimens, however, have been found with as few as 4 eggs.

North American Venomous Snakes
Copperhead
Agkistrodon contortrix

It's easy to see how the North American copperhead acquired its name: the unpatterned head is coppery red in the North, paler or even pinkish with a coppery tinge in the South. Its ground color is reddish or hazel brown, offset with a series of darker chestnut or chocolate brown crossbands that look like hourglasses or dumbbells. The contrasting shades, Morris observes, "have been likened to the contrast between an old copper penny and a shiny new one." (The Australian copperhead, no relation, earned its name the same way.)

During the Civil War, the word "copperhead" had a different meaning: a Northerner (or Southerner residing in the North) who sympathized with the Confederate cause. Historians often claim the nickname evolved from the parallel between the "treacherous" copperhead snake (a species that blends in superbly with its habitat and ambushes its prey) and the traitorous Southern sympathizers.

In truth, the original Copperheads were members of patriotic societies such as the Knights of the Golden Circle and Sons of Liberty who identified themselves by

Copperhead

The cryptic coloration and hourglass-patterned crossbands of the venomous North American copperhead blend in perfectly with fall leaves on the floor of hardwood forests. A copperhead tracks its prey by picking up scent particles with its two-pronged tongue. The feeding habits of this snake are apparently seasonal: frogs are preferred in the spring and fall, while fledgling birds are favored in late spring and small rodents in summer.

Copperheads account for a large share of the venomous snakebites reported in the United States.

holding out a copper coin with the head side up. Furthermore, the label apparently existed long before it was applied to the renegades from Dixie: it had been used disparagingly for Native Americans and for the Dutch inhabitants of New York.

Historically, some Americans claimed the handsome, though venomous copperhead is wicked, vicious, and ill-tempered, while others argue it is unusually even-tempered and as likely to glide away as it is to defend itself. The Southern copperhead has "an inoffensive disposition and [is] little likely to bite anyone who does not actually interfere with it," North Carolina naturalist Clement Brimley once remarked. "Specimens that I have had in captivity have seemed so tame that it appeared I could have handled them with impunity, *if I had been fool enough to take the risk.*"

And risk there is: the five subspecies of copperheads—Northern, Southern, Trans-Pecos, Osage, and broad-banded—account for a large share of the venomous snakebites reported in the United States. Fortunately, mortality is "almost nonexistent," Ernst reports, and most bites occur when these snakes are being handled, or when they are stepped on or touched accidentally. Luckily, copperhead fangs are shorter than those of most rattlesnakes.

When alarmed, many copperheads vibrate their tails rapidly like rattlesnakes and some nonvenomous snakes, producing a warning buzz in dry leaves. If restrained, the snake will "fight furiously," Ditmars says, thrashing its body from side to side and sometimes unintentionally "inflicting a wound upon itself." If picked up, the snake may leave an aromatic calling card: a musky secretion likened to the smell of cucumbers.

But these serpents would prefer to get out of harm's way, which is why Ernst and Barbour boast that "copperheads are better lovers than fighters." As Henry Fitch describes it, a copperhead courtship ritual can be quite animated: "The male moved toward [the female] and came into contact . . . then became moderately excited and began to rub his chin along her body in short spasmodic jerks . . . rapidly protruding his tongue. . . . [The male] placed the posterior part of his body alongside and forced it under the female with a rippling movement. When the female began to crawl, the male became extremely active and moved his entire body convulsively."

A pair of mating copperheads may remain together for as long as eight hours, which perhaps discourages other males from approaching the female and attempting to mate. During this interlude, males may produce a pheromone that "makes females unattractive to other males," Tyning reports. Like many rattlesnakes, male copperheads engage in ritualistic combat dances, swaying rhythmically and attempting to pin or "top" the head of their rival. Explanations for this behavior include mating competition, food competition, and territoriality.

Gravid females often come together in so-called birthing rookeries, sharing available space in logs or rock piles, where they give birth to four to eight young. To slit their way through their transparent membrane, baby copperheads use an egg tooth, which they later discard. The tips of their tails are a brilliant sulfur yellow or lettuce green, just like those of newborn cottonmouths; when twisted and wriggled, the tail tips look like grubs or maggots and attract prey.

Copperheads eat a variety of insects, amphibians, reptiles, birds, and small

Copperhead
This unusually patterned copperhead, photographed on cypress needles near Reelfoot Lake in west Tennessee, waits to ambush small prey. Many young copperheads have a yellow-tipped tail, which they point upward and move slowly to lure frogs, lizards, rodents, and small birds within striking range.

mammals, and field biologists have observed that their feeding habits can be seasonal: in the spring and fall, copperheads prefer frogs; during the late spring, young birds; and during the summer, small rodents.

The copperhead's appetite for cicadas accounts for sightings of this ordinarily terrestrial snake in shrubs and trees. Howard Gloyd and Roger Conant, citing records of copperheads with stomachs "stuffed" with these insects, note that in 1978 a field researcher along the Colorado River in Texas collected nearly one hundred copperheads from oak trees where cicadas were emerging from their skins. The snakes had climbed the trees—some as high as 40 feet (12 m)—by crawling up wild grapevines that encircled the trunks and branches.

More frequently, these medium-sized snakes, which average 2 to 3 feet (61 to 90 cm), are found among the fallen leaves of wooded or brushy areas, on hillsides near rocky ledges (where they are fond of basking in the sun), or in hay fields, orchards, blueberry thickets, and meadows.

Copperheads also turn up near or in human habitations throughout their range from New England west into Kansas and south into Texas. With artful camouflage, they blend in so well with stone walls, woodpiles, and old cellars that they generally go unseen. Kentucky native Alben Barkley was bitten by a copperhead at the age of six while crawling under his family's cabin in search of a chicken; he survived the bite and went on to serve as vice president of the United States under Harry Truman.

When alarmed, many copperheads vibrate their tails rapidly like rattlesnakes, producing a warning buzz in dry leaves.

Western Diamondback Rattlesnake
Crotalus atrox

"At the top of the list of rattlers quick to anger," Klauber wrote in his monumental two-volume study of rattlesnakes, "I should put the Western diamondback."

And that is just one of its claims to fame. The longest venomous snake in the American West, it reaches a record 7 feet 3½ inches (2.22 m) and is responsible for more fatal bites than any other North American species. Stebbins calls it "perhaps the most dangerous North American serpent," and Ditmars once rated it "the second most formidable serpent of North America" after its relative, the Eastern diamondback.

Bold by nature and quick to assume the S-shaped defensive coil with head raised as high as 20 inches (50 cm), individuals not only hold their ground but sometimes advance toward intruders. Never hesitant to rattle its tail when alarmed or provoked, the Western diamondback sometimes drapes a coil of its body over the rattle while waiting to ambush prey, perhaps to muffle the sound. In some locales, this snake is known as the "coontail rattler," an apparent reference to the distinctive black and whitish-gray rings above the rattle.

The diamondback's coloration is generally cinnamon brown or limestone gray, though sometimes pink or yellowish, with a series of reddish or dark brown diamond-shaped markings down the back. The keeled scales have a dusty appearance, "often matching or blending with the soil color of the area in which a given population occurs," John Mehrtens observes. Over the prominent vertical pupil of the eye can be seen a stripe or mask that extends to the corner of the mouth.

The venom of this formidable rattlesnake attacks the blood cells, Ernst explains, causing rapid hemorrhaging from breakdown of vascular tissues. Due to the high venom yield, surpassed in the United States only by the Eastern diamondback, "this snake is not one to be messed with," he warns. Its fangs have been measured at an impressive 0.57 inch (1.45 cm) across the curve in a 5-foot (1.5 m) specimen. Contrary to legend, this snake is not immune to the venom of other Western diamondbacks.

Field biologists have discovered Western diamondbacks in a wide variety of habitats, from arid and semiarid regions (including deserts, mesquite groves, prickly-pear cactus thickets, dry riverbeds, canyons, and mountains) to prairies, shrublands, pine forests, and dense woodlands. Western diamondbacks also turn up in fields and pastures, scrap heaps, woodpiles, and on roads at night. Because they overwinter together in great numbers (Klauber cites reports of as many as two hundred Western diamondbacks in a single winter den), populations are easily located and decimated by fanatical hunters seeking victims for annual "rattlesnake roundups" in Texas, Oklahoma, and elsewhere. Many rattlers are also killed off as part of a thriving export trade to Asia, and to provide exotic fare for gourmet restaurants.

Regrettably, the diamondback's rattle—which probably evolved as a warning mechanism to keep larger animals from stepping on the snake, or as a biochemical response to stress—is prized as a trophy by too many humans; in Western states, these rattles adorn wall panels, ten-gallon hats, and bizarre desktop curios. Contrary to popular belief, strings of rattles do *not* indicate the age of an individual snake; though one rattle is added every time the snake sheds its skin, long strings are sub-

The Western diamondback rattlesnake is the longest venomous snake in the American West, reaching a record 7 feet 3½ inches (2.22 m)

ject to wear and tear in the wild and frequently break apart. Lightning-fast tail vibrations—as many as 90 per second—create the familiar buzzing sound of the diamondback's rattle string.

Chiefly but not exclusively nocturnal, Western diamondbacks find their prey by active foraging or by lying in ambush, often beside a rodent trail. Kangaroo rats, ground squirrels, gophers, rabbits, lizards, snakes, and birds are favored prey. Enemies—besides humans—include badgers, bobcats, skunks, roadrunners, owls, hawks, wild turkeys, and several species of snakes.

Western diamondbacks mate in the fall and at other times of the year. Copulation can last anywhere from fifteen minutes to eight hours, and amorous males have been known to pursue females single-mindedly past human observers and even between their legs. Like other rattlesnakes, male diamondbacks engage in combat dances, rearing up and entwining their sinuous bodies, attempting to force an opponent to the ground until it concedes defeat. Females give birth to four to twenty-three live young.

Generally, Western diamondbacks are found from western Arkansas through Texas to southeastern California and northern Mexico, but a curator of reptiles at the Milwaukee Public Museum reported that several Western diamondbacks escaped from a circus in western Wisconsin around 1920, and at least one was a gravid female. The diamondbacks became established, Ditmars recounts, "and spread for many miles along the shattered cliffs, indicating adaptation to endure the long and severe winters of Wisconsin." (Robert Henderson, the museum's current curator, says there have been no reports of diamondbacks in recent years.)

Black-Tailed Rattlesnake
Crotalus molossus

Over the years, many observers have characterized the black-tailed rattler as America's most handsome rattlesnake. With a rich sulfur yellow, greenish yellow, or olive green body color (hence the nickname green rattler), this snake is recognized by its trademark charcoal black tail, single-colored scales (other North American rattlers have mostly mottled scales on their backs), a black or chocolate-colored mask over the snout, and a series of brown or black dorsal crossbands, diamonds, or rhomboidal blotches. The result, Tennant suggests, is a "striking light-and-dark motif" whose lines suggest the patterns of Navajo beadwork.

Ranging from central Texas into southern New Mexico and western Arizona, as well as western Mexico and islands in the Gulf of California, this snake turns up in

*W*estern diamondback rattlesnakes are responsible for more fatal bites than any other North American species.

Western diamondback rattlesnake

The Western diamondback is an irascible, often aggressive species, quick to stand its ground and vibrate its tail. Authorities report that the formidable fangs and copious venom of this rattlesnake are responsible for more fatalities than any other North American serpent.

Eastern diamondback rattlesnake

The Eastern diamondback is the largest venomous snake in the United States, reaching a record 8 feet (243.8 cm) in length. Though extremely dangerous, this rattlesnake has a relatively mild temperament, often lying quietly without moving when first discovered.

to rattle at the slightest disturbance." Tennant found that certain individuals were "hot-tempered" and struck at the screen tops of their cages "whenever a shadow passed overhead." One large female would fling herself against the thick glass front of her enclosure every time her keeper walked by with a lit cigarette, prompting the conclusion that the glowing ember triggered the snake's thermoreceptive pits.

Unlike other rattlesnakes, Tennant reports, this species extends its long black tongue "far back over the snout" and rests it on the crown of its head for several minutes at a time. Because the head is large and blunt, this snake is sometimes called a dog-faced or dog-headed rattlesnake. The largest specimen on record is a 52-inch (1.32 m) individual collected by Texas wildlife wardens; the average length, however, is 28 to 42 inches (0.7 to 1.07 m).

Black-tailed rattlers are customarily found in canyons or rocky areas near cliffs—often in talus slides, under boulders, around rocky outcrops, or near abandoned mine shafts—and in terrain dotted with scrub and cactus. They are remarkably cold-tolerant, and some have been observed emerging from their hibernacula to bask during brief warm spells in January and February. During the spring and fall, these snakes are chiefly diurnal, but during the hot summer months they prefer to hunt their prey—mice, wood rats, rock squirrels, birds, and lizards—late at night. Females give birth to litters of three to six young during the summer.

Although black-tailed rattlesnakes usually retreat to a crevice or rocky cover when a human approaches, some rattle their tails violently or gape with an open mouth for as long as five minutes to warn or intimidate an intruder. Due to the relative inac-

a variety of colors and patterns. Silvery or brown color morphs are prevalent throughout the Trans-Pecos region of Texas, and specimens found on lava flows are often melanistic (black), presumably an adaptation to their dark habitat. When viewed in just the right light, this species may exhibit a blue, purplish, or greenish iridescence.

Personalities, like colors, can vary widely. Kauffeld once kept a black-tailed rattlesnake that exhibited a "completely phlegmatic" disposition: it was impassive and "very calm," except when put on display. "He was the exception to the rule that black-taileds are irritable and prone

cessibility of their habitat, these snakes seldom come into contact with people, so bites are rare. Their fangs are relatively long, however, and their venom can cause serious hemorrhaging.

When Harry Greene and David L. Hardy, Sr., planted radiotelemetric devices in black-tailed rattlers in southwestern Arizona, they found themselves surprised by some of the idiosyncrasies of their snakes. "Number 8 unsuccessfully courted a female in a small tree," Greene recalls, and courting pairs remained together "for days." Sometimes fights broke out when another suitor materialized and approached a courting pair. And Number 12, Greene chuckles, "had a thing for chipmunks."

Tiger Rattlesnake
Crotalus tigris

The tiger rattlesnake of North America may not have the temperament of its carnivorous Asian namesake, but it shares at least one important feature: stripes. It also sports a conspicuously long tail (or, more accurately, rattle string) and a tawny ground color, which blends in well with the rocky landscape it inhabits.

The multiplicity of crossbands (anywhere from thirty-five to fifty-two) may have given this species its name, but the markings are not necessarily distinct like a tiger's. The gray or brown bands are composed of a series of dots or "smoky darkenings," often blotchy and ill defined, which contrast background colors that range from yellow, orange, or brown to blue gray, lavender, or pink. The underside of the snake is straw-colored or olive buff, and the eyes are cinnamon or pink, flecked with gray.

Unlike most of its rattlesnake kin, the tiger rattler is a relatively "new" species,

unreported until the 1850s, when a member of the U.S. and Mexican Boundary Survey discovered one on the Sonoran border of northwestern Mexico. (The timber rattlesnake, in contrast, had been recorded as early as 1634.)

The moderate-sized tiger rattler, which averages 2½ to 3 feet (about 76 to 91 cm), is found in the desert mountains, rocky foothills, and canyons of south-central Arizona southward through Sonora, Mexico, where mesquite, creosote bushes, and saguaro and ocotillo cactus flourish. The limited range and remoteness of the tiger rattler's habitat have kept it well isolated, and its relatively placid disposition may have helped it to remain incognito.

Despite its particularly large rattle, the tiger rattlesnake "usually greets danger with camouflaged silence," Robert Gaulden writes, and it prefers to "bolt" into rocky crevices when it perceives a threat. Human encounters are relatively rare—which is just as well, since the venom is extraordinarily potent.

The tiger rattlesnake is probably the most dangerous serpent north of Mexico, as its venom has up to twenty times the killing power of the Western diamondback's venom.

Black-tailed rattlesnake
The black-tailed rattler inhabits rocky canyons, semiarid foothills with cactus and brush, and broken wooded terrain of the American Southwest and Mexico. These robust snakes are distinguished by a sooty black tail and a solid stripe behind the eye.

Tiger rattlesnake
The tiger rattlesnake has cinnamon-pink eyes and a pinkish, tawny ground color with smoky crossbands made up of dark dots. Especially active after warm summer rains, this placid rattlesnake is restricted to dry, rocky canyons and mesquite grasslands of the Sonoran Desert.

"Drop for drop," Gaulden reports, the tiger rattler's venom "delivers up to twenty times the killing power of Western diamondback venom" and "approximates the potency of the Mojave rattler's" (the latter, Tennant says, is "probably the most dangerous serpent north of Mexico" and has a lethal potential "unequaled in this country"). The venom yield for this species is so small, however, that it cannot inflict the damage of a Mojave or Western diamondback rattlesnake. The reason for the mod-est venom yield, herpetologists suspect, is the tiger's small, narrow head.

Gaulden speculates that the narrow head may offer an advantage to a predator that lives in rocky, rugged terrain: when the snake pursues a mouse or lizard that tries to wedge itself into a crack, he explains, "the tiger rattlesnake's small head operates as a pair of tweezers for extracting the prey."

Tiger rattlers engage in nocturnal or diurnal activity, depending on the season and temperature, although they are most likely to emerge from their rocky retreats after a warm rain shower—especially in September, when heavy rains produce monsoon-like conditions. Though considered relatively rare, this snake demonstrates an almost catlike ability to appear and disappear.

Pigmy Rattlesnake
Sistrurus miliarius

The pigmy rattlesnake, a.k.a. the "buzzworm," is a small species found in the southeastern United States that averages just 15 to 21 inches (38 to 53 cm). Like its larger rattlesnake brethren, the pigmy is equipped with a rattle, but the individual segments are very small and together produce only a faint buzzing sound—"more like that of an insect than a rattlesnake," says Mattison. Their tails are relatively long and slender and rarely have rattle strings with more than six rattles.

Researchers at Appalachian State University have recorded, digitized, and analyzed the rattling sounds of some twenty-one different species of rattlesnakes and found that pigmy rattlers produce much fainter and higher-pitched sounds than other rattlesnakes. Patrick Cook and his colleagues believe the diminutive rattles may have evolved not as warning devices but rather as lures, attracting prey by mimicking worms or grubs. Juveniles are born with a more prominent tail tip—generally sulfur yellow or white—which attracts potential prey.

Adult pigmy rattlers are less vividly marked overall than juveniles and are generally gray to ashy gray, or brown to reddish brown. But the pride of the pigmy rattlesnake clan, the Carolina pigmy rattlesnake, boasts a gorgeous brick red, orangish, or pinkish ground color, offset with irregular blotches or bands down the center of its back. This subspecies ranges from Hyde County, North Carolina, and neighboring counties southwest into central Georgia and Alabama; other pigmy rattlers are found from the central and southeastern United States west to Oklahoma.

Often found under leaf litter or bark in loblolly-pine, scrub-oak, or palmetto woods, Carolina pigmy rattlers feed on lizards, snakes, and small birds and mammals; unlike most rattlesnakes, however, they also consume insects and spiders, as well as their favorite prey—frogs. The venom of pigmy rattlers is "fairly toxic," Mattison reports, but because their fangs are short, they are unable to penetrate deeply.

For such a diminutive snake, this species has an unusually fiery temper, Ernst observes, and it throws its body into a

The pigmy rattlesnake is also known as the "buzzworm."

Pigmy rattlesnake
Many pigmy rattlesnakes, especially newborns, are feisty and hot-tempered, striking repeatedly if disturbed. The rattles on their tails are so tiny they produce only a faint sound, easily mistaken for an insect's buzzing.

Carolina pigmy rattlesnake
The Carolina, or red, pigmy rattlesnake of eastern North Carolina has more vibrant shades of red and orange than other pigmy subspecies. Although its venom yield is small and its short fangs cannot penetrate deeply, this snake has a relatively toxic venom and should be avoided.

fighting coil and strikes with vicious, repeated jabs. When accosted, it sometimes bobs its head and moves its tail erratically.

Researcher Peter May and his associates at Stetson University have tracked dusky pigmy rattlesnakes implanted with small microchips and found that males perform a "mate-guarding behavior" by remaining close to reproductive females "for extended periods of time . . . often with one snake coiled on top of the other for several days." Females apparently store the male sperm until the spring of the following year, when fertilization takes place. The five to eighteen live young "remain tightly clustered within a few feet of their mother for several days after birth," May et al. report.

Unlike many rattlers, pigmies apparently do not migrate or congregate at winter hibernacula, preferring instead to retreat individually under available debris and shallow cover. Once commonly known as the "ground rattler," the pigmy rattler has been discovered on branches and palm fronds—reportedly up to several feet above ground.

Evolutionary biologist Edward O. Wilson recalls that pigmy rattlesnakes were his "star attractions" when he was a nature counselor at a Boy Scout camp in Alabama. But one day, "in a moment of carelessness," he moved a hand too close to one of his snakes, and it bit him on the tip of his index finger.

Whisked off to the town doctor for the standard treatment for snakebite, Wilson didn't cry, he relates in his autobiography. "I held my hand steady and cursed loudly nonstop with four-letter words, at myself for my stupidity and not at the innocent doctor or the snake. . . . It was a bad time for herpetology at Camp Pushmataha. When I returned to resume my duties"—

after a weeklong convalescence at home—"I found that the camp supervisor had wisely disposed of the pigmy rattlesnakes."

International Rear-Fanged and Venomous Snakes
Asian Vine Snake
Ahaetulla nasuta

"As you were when first your eye I ey'd / Such seems your beauty still," William Shakespeare gushed in one of his later sonnets. Although not a herpetologist (despite an interest in eye of newt and toe of frog), Shakespeare might easily have been rhapsodizing over the eye of the Asian vine snake, a species of great beauty known by a confusing litany of names: Asian long-nosed snake, long-nosed vine snake, long-nosed tree snake, Oriental whipsnake, and green whipsnake.

This serpent—a native of India, Sri Lanka, and Southeast Asia—not only has eyes considerably larger than most snakes', but also uniquely shaped pupils. While virtually all reptiles and amphibians have round or elliptical pupils, the Asian vine snake has a keyhole-shaped pupil, characterized by one biologist as "a small figure eight lying on its side."

According to Harvey Lillywhite and Robert Henderson, the horizontal keyhole "widens the binocular field without compromising the extent of periscopy," allowing the snake to judge distances with remarkable accuracy. In most snakes, the overlapping field of vision is approximately 30°; in arboreal species such as vine snakes, it approaches 46°.

The elongated snout of this species is believed to be an evolutionary modification that enhances vision. Two grooves along the snout in front of the eyes minimize nasal obstruction and extend the eye line for sighting prey, enabling the snake "to pick out cryptically colored lizards that otherwise would not be visible within the environment," Peter Brazaitis and Myrna Watanabe write. This evolutionary advantage is particularly significant, since vine snakes are among the few species apparently able to detect motionless prey—chiefly geckos and other lizards.

While the eye and snout make this snake unique, other traits command attention as well. Well suited to an arboreal environment where their leaf-green coloration provides excellent camouflage, their long, slender bodies are easily mistaken for rain forest vines. In addition, "when the wind blows, they sway their bodies like branches," says herpetologist J. L. Cloudsley-Thompson. "Some species even fall to the ground when touched and lie motionless there, looking like dead twigs."

Achieving an average length of about 4½ feet (1.4 cm), the vine snake's long, slim body is well adapted to moving along slender branches and bridging gaps between them, as well as capturing prey on unstable surfaces such as leaves and twigs. Unlike adults, which generally lie across branches, newborn vine snakes sometimes wrap their bodies around branches, Robert Henderson and Mary Binder note. Female vine snakes give birth to litters of three to twenty-two offspring at a time, reportedly at almost any time during the year.

When this diurnal snake encounters a predator, it gapes menacingly, displaying the startling black interior of its mouth. When angered, it often thrusts out a rigid tongue and inflates its body, exposing black interstitial skin between the green scales.

Although not considered dangerous to humans, the Asian vine snake is a rear-

Asian vine snakes not only have eyes larger than most snakes' but also uniquely shaped pupils that look like keyholes.

fanged species with enlarged teeth at the back of its mouth; when it bites it holds onto its prey, immobilizing the victim with its venom. Humans bitten by vine snakes sometimes report localized swelling, numbness, and pain.

Mangrove Snake
Boiga dendrophila

The mangrove snake is a deceptively beautiful denizen of the mangrove swamps and rain forests of the Malay Peninsula and Sumatra. With satiny-smooth black scales and bands of vivid yellow, its skin is so glossy it looks "freshly painted," Ditmars observes. Because its large eyes and vertically slit pupils resemble those of a cat, it's no wonder this serpent is often called a cat snake.

While the mangrove snake's handsome appearance contributes to its current popularity, its quick response when startled also fascinates observers. Gaping fiercely, this snake displays the unnerving rosy-pink lining of its mouth and usually accompanies the gape with feints and actual lunges.

Inside that conspicuously exposed mouth is a set of large rear fangs, which channel venom down grooves along the teeth to quickly immobilize and kill small prey. The venom, described variously as "dangerous" or "slightly dangerous" to man, has been responsible for several cases of envenomation in humans. In one incident, a Malayan snake catcher bitten on the shoulder by a large mangrove snake promptly fainted, fell to the ground, and spent a week in the hospital.

There is some debate whether the gaping behavior and bright glossy bands should be regarded as a bluff or threat. Some scientists believe the bright yellow

Mangrove snakes grow up to 6 to 8 feet (1.8 to 2.4 m) in length.

Asian vine snake

Lying motionless on a rain forest tree limb, the rear-fanged Asian vine snake detects prey with its extraordinary sense of vision, enhanced by horizontal keyhole-shaped pupils and grooves along the snout in front of the eyes.

Mangrove snake

The mangrove snake's glistening black skin, bright yellow bands, catlike pupils, and intense gaping displays fascinate zoogoers and hobbyists, but this handsome tree snake's rear fangs and venom are considered dangerous to man.

bands are an example of Batesian mimicry, whereby this "harmless" species enhances its survival chances by mimicking the patterns of several venomous Malayan kraits with similar black, white, and yellow bands.

Mangrove snakes grow quite long—6 to 8 feet (1.8 to 2.4 m)—and may spend virtually their entire lives in trees. Agile climbers, they coil on tree limbs and hang over rivers and streams, hunting at night for birds, bats, rodents, frogs, lizards, and snakes. Females lay seven to ten eggs, of-

ten in the hollow of a tree. In Jakarta, snake catchers pluck them from trees and sell them to local dealers, who use the snakes for medicinal and culinary purposes.

Horned Viper
Cerastes cerastes

When animal lovers are asked to name species with horns, they usually cite rhinos and bighorn sheep, hornbills and great horned owls, or even "horned toads." They seldom think of horns on snakes.

Yet, surprisingly, many serpents around the world—sidewinders, adders, and vipers—have interesting hornlike spines (scales) that jut from their heads. While several have raised spines on their snout, the African horned viper and others sport an enlarged, erect hornlike scale over each eye. Although their function remains the subject of debate, their position on the viper's brow certainly bestows a dragonlike majesty.

In the fine sand of the Sahara and dry regions of the Arabian Peninsula, these vipers may have evolved horns to protect their eyes from sand or soil. John Mehrtens notes that the horns keep sand from piling up over the eyes and restricting vision after the viper buries itself with only its horns left exposed and waits to ambush prey. The horns may also be useful in protecting the eyes from sun, Stidworthy says, or they could be "a natural trip device," Brazaitis and Watanabe suggest. African snake expert R. M. Isemonger once speculated the horns may serve as bait to attract birds and small animals.

Crossing the shifting sands with what Greene calls a "bizarre, rolling crawl," the African horned viper has developed a curious method for sinking into the substrate. Body scales on the snake's sides have angled, serrated keels that "remove sand from beneath the snake," Mehrtens explains, "simultaneously placing it over the snake's body, whose rocking action sets the entire process in motion." When rubbed together, these rough, keeled scales produce a loud rasping sound, similar to that of the saw-scaled viper. This peculiar behavior, Mattison suggests, "may have evolved because the snakes live in arid habitats . . . where water is precious. If they were to hiss, they would lose water, in the form of vapour, as the air was expelled through their mouth."

Although the venom of the horned viper can be deadly, few fatalities have been recorded, probably because this creature is nocturnal and has limited contact with humans. In 1901, Hans Gadow reported that horned vipers appeared "in perplexing numbers" at campfires, apparently attracted to the heat, and Nobel Peace Prize winner Albert Schweitzer frequently encountered horned vipers at his West African hospital camp.

"We are afraid of it not only because its bite is dangerous," Schweitzer wrote, "but also because it is so inconspicuous. One may discover other snakes when they take to flight or rear up to defend themselves, but the horned viper remains so still at the approach of a person that one may sometimes step over it without its moving. But

Many serpents around the world—including sidewinders, adders, and vipers—have hornlike spines that jut from their heads.

Horned viper

The horned viper of northern Africa and the Arabian peninsula has a prominent "horn"—actually a ribbed scale—over each eye. These vipers bury themselves in sand with just their eyes and horns exposed, escaping extreme heat while lying in wait for unsuspecting lizards.

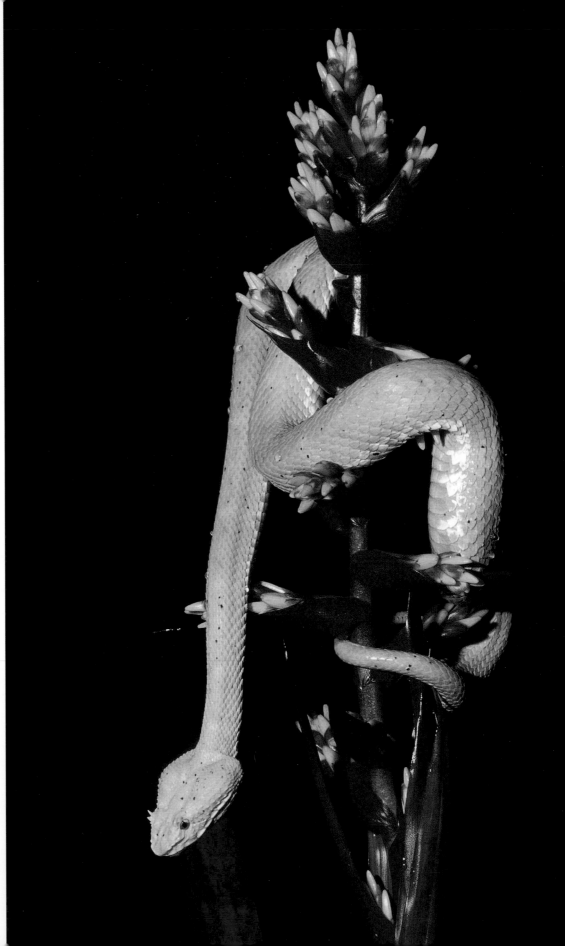

Eyelash vipers' fangs are excessively long, allowing the snake to grab a bird in flight with its open mouth.

Eyelash viper

The brilliant yellow of some eyelash vipers offers excellent camouflage when the snake coils around ripe palm fruit or bright tropical flowers to ambush hummingbirds. From time to time, these vipers have turned up in shipments of bananas to New York and other cities.

if one alarms or disturbs it, it will strike with a terrifying rapidity that allows no escape."

Female horned vipers lay up to twenty-five eggs, which they bury in abandoned burrows or beneath rocks. The species grows to a maximum of about 30 inches (76.2 cm), with an average length of 20 to 25 inches (50.8 to 63.5 cm). Like the sidewinder of the American Southwest—a desert-dwelling pit viper that resembles the horned viper in color, size, and horns—the horned viper has a ground color that varies from yellowish or sandy brown to pale gray or pinkish, with dark spots down the back that sometimes fuse into crossbars, matching the sand of the desert habitat.

Eyelash Viper
Bothriechis schlegelii

"False gold." That's what explorers in Central America called the stunning but dangerous viper with the remarkable golden skin. Known today as the eyelash viper or eyelash palm-pitviper, this serpent is found in three distinct color phases—bright lemon yellow or burnished gold; olive green or lichen, flecked with red, brown, and black; and salmon pink or rust. (Some specimens are even orange, tan, blue, or purple.)

Of the three principal color morphs, the glowing yellow is probably the most handsome—and "about as easy to overlook as a neon sign," Weidensaul declares. Once plentiful in banana groves, these snakes would conceal themselves in bunches of bananas and occasionally reach ports in the United States after stowing away in fruit shipments from Honduras, Nicaragua, Costa Rica, and Panama. Herpetologist Charles Bogert recalls a man being bitten in the 1950s by an eyelash viper that arrived

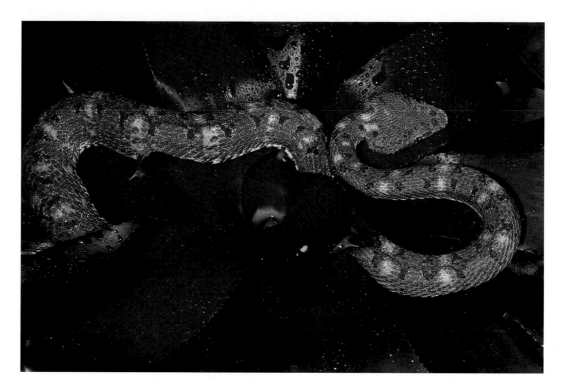

in New York City in a banana shipment, and Sherman and Madge Minton remember a wholesale fruit dealer in Indianapolis who used to show up at the local medical school with exotic tropical specimens, including one eyelash viper. "Today, bananas are treated with so many sprays and dips," they note, "that very few animals survive."

Eyelash vipers are persistently arboreal, usually spotted in vine tangles, shrubbery, low trees, or at the base of palm stems. Fieldworkers on banana and cacao plantations encountered these snakes regularly, and Ditmars warned prospectors and trail gangs to be "wary" of bushy areas where men were fatally bitten. (Young snakes, born in litters of six to twelve, accounted for more than one-third of the bites.) While the cryptic coloration offers camouflage among ripening bananas, it may have evolved to mimic yellow palm fruit or even bright tropical flowers.

Eyelash viper
One color morph of the eyelash viper has a lichen-green body color speckled with red and black flecks. Relatively short and chunky, this viper has a large head with hornlike scales above the eye and long fangs capable of delivering a fatal bite.

Distinctive spiny or hornlike scales above the conspicuous vertical pupils give the snake its name, but eyelash viper is just one of many vernacular names. Another familiar label, Schlegel's viper, honors the German naturalist Hermann Schlegel.

Eyelash vipers are relatively short, averaging 16 to 24 inches (41 to 61 cm), although individuals have been known to reach 31 inches (80 cm). Their fangs, in contrast, are quite long ("excessively long," says one herpetologist) and critical to their success as predators: winding its prehen-

sile tail around a branch, the snake "grabs at birds with its open mouth while dangling in the air," Carr notes. After making a successful pass, the snake holds the prey firmly with its long fangs and waits for the venom to take effect.

Once, on a soggy trip down the Amazon, writer Alex Shoumatoff heard some small birds screeching hysterically in a nearby tree and saw "the bright emerald ribbon" of an eyelash viper "slipping along the branch to the nest." His guide explained that the nocturnal snakes often come out

Gaboon viper

The colorful geometrical patterns of Gaboon vipers, with purple and brown ground colors and hourglass rings or blotches of light yellow or blue, invite comparison to Oriental carpets. The gaudy colors, large nasal "horns," and huge fangs inspired Ditmars to call this "the world's most frightful-looking snake."

after a rainstorm or shower.

"*Mordeu, morreu,*" shuddered the guide. "If you are bitten, you die."

Gaboon Viper
Bitis gabonica

It has been called the world's most "frightful-looking" snake, the most "awe-inspiring serpent alive," and the one snake that "comes closest to delivering 'sudden death.'" Ditmars, Pope, and Caras should know—they all had firsthand encounters with Gaboon vipers during their lives.

To the average zoogoer, however, the Gaboon viper or adder may resemble an overstuffed sausage, heavy and flattened, decorated like an Oriental rug. So sleepy-looking that they appear incapable of making fast movements, these vipers have a way of surprising people—as curator of reptiles Marlin Perkins discovered when he was bitten by a large Gaboon viper at the St. Louis Zoological Gardens. Struck on the left index finger by a single fang while treating a specimen for parasites, Perkins soon experienced difficulty breathing, his pulse weakened until it could no longer be felt, and he lapsed into unconsciousness after one hour. In fact, he probably would have died had Ditmars not advised immediate injection of cobra serum and a fer-de-lance/ *Bothrops* polyvalent (multispecies) antivenom after the initial injection of an American polyvalent antivenom proved insufficient.

Although stout-bodied with a stubby tail and a languid appearance, the Gaboon viper can inflict serious blood and tissue damage, or cause death, because of the extraordinary length of its hinged front fangs—up to 1½ inches (38 mm), perhaps the longest of any snake. These fangs penetrate deeply, and some vipers hold onto their prey after biting instead of withdrawing.

To observers, this snake is a paradox. While some specimens have a "good-natured" or "mild" disposition and are slow to take offense when disturbed, others lash out instinctively at any intruder perceived as a threat. In all likelihood, they hiss noisily and lunge at enemies because their hefty body weight—some weigh close to 20 pounds (9 kg)—makes a retreat relatively slow.

The Gaboon viper, a resident of central African rain forests, only becomes active around sunset, so it is seldom encountered by humans. Ironically, it remains a threat because it is so difficult to see by day: the skin patterns render the snake nearly invisible on a leaf-covered forest floor and thus vulnerable to being stepped on. Hubert Saint-Girons compares the viper's "magnificent" pattern to "those seen on ornate Oriental carpets" and adds: "the deep purple-brown background has geometrical patterns in yellow, light brown, and blue, usually in an hourglass arrangement along the sides, with long, rectangular, deep-purple bordered rings."

Relying on its cryptic pattern for camouflage, this slow-moving but relatively large viper (some measure longer than 5½ feet, or 1.65 m) typically ambushes rather than stalks its prey, feeding chiefly on small mammals and birds—and, in at least one instance, a small antelope.

Mambas
Dendroaspis

In John Godey's 1978 novel *The Snake*, a large black mamba escapes in New York's Central Park and the city goes haywire. When dining out, New Yorkers begin lifting tablecloths to check for the snake; oth-

Green mambas can grow to 10 feet (3.05 m); the record length for a black mamba is 13 feet 7 inches (4.14 m).

ers walk out of plays and concerts early, "because they kept imagining snakes crawling around their feet in the darkness." Many fear their apartments or cars might harbor the snake, "and all over the city, people took to sitting in chairs with their feet tucked under them."

Mambas can have that sort of effect on people—even in real life.

The four species of this serpent (three green mambas and the black mamba) are greatly feared throughout eastern and south central Africa, yet, despite their sinister reputation and widely celebrated speed, they cause relatively few fatalities.

After observing mambas in Africa, Carr characterized the snakes as "big, swift, obstreperous, and even warlike." He wasn't kidding. Green mambas can grow to 10 feet (3.05 m), and the record length for a black mamba is 13 feet 7 inches (4.14 m). Mambas "may well be the fastest of all snakes," Sherman and Madge Minton write; "reliable observers have estimated their top speed at twenty miles an hour."

After opening his first shipment of mambas at the New York Zoological Park, Ditmars accidentally poked one of the eight new snakes with a long rod. "I have never noted a quicker movement on the part of a snake," he recalled. "Its full length came through the door with a speed looking like the shaft of a traveling arrow."

The Nashville Zoo's curator of reptiles, Dale McGinnity, confirms that these snakes are swift and uncooperative. A western (or West African) green mamba that he raised from a baby and that now measures 7 to 8 feet (about 2.13 to 2.44 m) "has a mind of its own," he says, adding that mambas are the "meanest and most aggressive" snakes and have "no fear of people." He characterizes his zoo's specimen as not

only "really smart" but also "the scariest snake I've ever dealt with." For this reason he takes special precautions with its quarters and has screwed down the air vent in the snake's glass cage "with about twenty screws. I was pretty anal about that."

Herpetologist Bill Haast, who at one time had 195 mambas at his Miami Serpentarium and still milks mambas at his laboratory in Punta Gorda, Florida, told an interviewer after he was twice bitten by green mambas, "They're like wound-up coils of steel all the time. Most snakes will tend to slide away, but if the mamba thinks he's cornered and wants to come out, he'll shoot out and won't hesitate to bite as he goes. He can do anything without any stance or pose."

Despite their fearsome reputation, there is no questioning their physical beauty. The vivid emerald green of the Western green mamba, Eastern green mamba, and Jameson's mamba has inspired some herpetologists to call this one of the most beautiful snakes in the world. "Its green is indescribable," Maurice Richardson marvels, and the snake "gives you a feeling of mystical exhilaration."

The black mamba, on the other hand, isn't even black: it received its name from the black, or blue black, color of the lining of its mouth (the body is gunmetal gray or olive brown). To complicate matters, juvenile black mambas are green, which for years caused them to be confused with green mambas. All mambas have unusually large eyes, with a round pupil and brown or gilded iris.

For a serpent of such unusual length ("mamba" is derived from the Zulu word for "big snake"), mambas have remarkably slender bodies, often not much thicker than a man's thumb. Older individuals, the

The name "mamba" is derived from the Zulu word for "big snake."

Western green mamba
The Western green mamba is an extremely slender tree climber that gapes in a threatening manner when startled, exposing the bluish white lining of its mouth. This African snake's large fangs are capable of injecting an exceptionally potent venom.

Western green mamba

Characteristic of a green mamba's eyes are large round pupils and a gilded iris. Less aggressive than black mambas, these vivid green serpents usually flee if given a chance, projecting themselves "like green arrows," according to one witness.

Mintons report, sometimes have difficulty shedding their skins, and the old slough may remain attached to the head, "forming a sort of plume or crest."

Some mambas are highly territorial and retreat regularly to the same tree hollows, aardvark burrows, or termite mounds. Green mambas are primarily arboreal, dwelling in mangrove forests, bamboo thickets, and tea plantations, while black mambas are more terrestrial, preferring animal holes or rocky outcrops near rivers.

In Zimbabwe, where the countryside is "riddled with long-forgotten mine shafts," Isemonger writes, many farmers have built outhouses over the deserted mine shafts.

Summoned to rid a farm of a pair of black mambas, Isemonger startled one with his noose, and it shot off in the direction of the antiquated outhouse, where the father of the family was "happily unaware of approaching danger. . . . My host was forced to vacate the building in such a hurry that he had to leave his trousers behind." After searching the rafters of the outhouse without success, Isemonger finally shone a flashlight down the shaft, where the beam illuminated a "distraught black mamba gazing up at us. Never before or since have I felt really sorry for a mamba."

During the breeding season, when males compete for mates by engaging in ritual-

ized fights (wrapping their bodies around one another and raising their heads threateningly), females lay anywhere from six to seventeen eggs. The "dark side" of this snake's personality is more likely to be glimpsed during the mating season, which perhaps explains contradictory reports of mamba behavior. Some field observers insist the snake is timid and nervous, fleeing at the approach of humans; others warn of its defensive, even aggressive, response. "Bus drivers stop if they see one on the road," says a South African commissioner, "for fear it may strike a passenger."

Since mambas have particularly large fangs, as well as enlarged teeth at the front of the lower jaw, which hold lizards, birds, and rodents while venom is injected, a bite suffered by a human can prove fatal if antivenom isn't administered swiftly. All mambas are capable of injecting more venom per bite, and more deeply, than a cobra.

Monocled Cobra
Naja kaouthia
"India swarms with deadly snakes," Mark Twain observed in Following the Equator. "At the head of the list is the cobra, the deadliest known to the world, a snake whose bite kills where the rattlesnake's bite merely entertains. . . . There are narrow escapes in India. In the very jungle where I killed sixteen tigers . . . a cobra bit me, but it got well; everyone was surprised."

Had he *really* been bitten by a cobra, Twain might not have joked so lightheartedly, since these snakes pose a very real threat to visiting humorists as well as to natives.

The distinctive markings visible on the spread hoods of several cobra species offer both an element of mystery and a connection to humans, who tend to anthropomorphize animals and "explain" nature's patterns. Both the Indian and Siamese cobra sport the familiar two-lensed "spectacle" on their hood—which a National Geographic writer once described as looking like the grin on a "clown's face"—while the monocled cobra has a single marking. Scientists point out that "monocled" is less accurate than "monocellated," and the hood marking is actually called an ocellus, or eyespot, like those on butterfly wings and peacock feathers.

According to legend, the monocle is the sign of Buddha, bestowed after he woke from a deep meditation at the side of a road. To shield him from the blistering sun, a cobra had spread its hood; in gratitude, Buddha gently kissed (or patted) the serpent, leaving an outline as a sign for the other creatures to see.

The monocled cobra's eyespot consists of a black ring or horseshoe-shaped mark enclosing a paler area with one or more spots in the center. These snakes are usually dark black or brown, or sometimes yellow, olive, or tan, and average 4 to 5 feet (about 1.2 to 1.5 m).

Monocled cobras are found in the lowlands of northeastern India, eastern Pakistan, Bangladesh, southwestern China, Burma, Thailand, and Vietnam, where they often turn up in villages and cities. They favor rice paddies, foundations of buildings, rock piles, termite mounds, and rodent burrows, where they prey on small mammals, birds, snakes, lizards, frogs, and toads.

Although the monocled cobra is equipped with "spitter" fangs for spraying venom at its enemies, Greene says it rarely spits. The true spitting varieties—which include the Javan, Chinese, Siamese,

According to legend, the cobra's monocle is the sign of Buddha.

123

The largest known king cobra was 18 feet 4 inches (5.58 m) in length.

Monocled cobra

The hood of a monocled cobra, spread when the snake is angered or excited, bears a single spectacle-like marking on the dorsal side. According to legend, the mark was created when Buddha kissed a cobra whose hood shielded him from the sun.

Sumatran, Mozambique, and black-necked spitting cobras and the rinkhals—aim for an adversary's eyes, where the venom, discharged along a spiral groove inside the fangs, causes extreme pain and spasms of the eyelids and can destroy eye tissues unless quickly washed out.

King Cobra
Ophiophagus hannah

Many a youngster's first impressions of the king cobra have probably been shaped by the swashbuckling accounts of animal collector-adventurer Frank Buck in his colorful 1930 autobiography, *Bring 'Em Back Alive*.

"The cobra alone," Buck wrote, "refuses to admit man is anything to worry about. Cross his path anywhere at any time and he'll raise off the ground, stretch out his great hood and go for you. There is a kind of horrible glamour about the unwillingness of this king of reptiles to make his peace with anyone or anything."

To illustrate, Buck recounted an incident in Singapore, where he was transferring a king cobra from a rickety cage into a new teakwood box. When a young assistant stumbled and jarred the cage, the rotting bottom fell out, and suddenly a 12½-foot (3.75-m) snake ("the largest king cobra I had ever seen . . . later proven to be the biggest in the world") fell onto the cement. Buck jumped just as the snake struck, and it missed his leg "by only an inch or two."

He discovered he was trapped.

"I suffered more from plain ordinary fright at that moment than at any time in all my long career of adventure," Buck confessed. "I didn't want to die this way. It was not my notion of a decent death."

His solution was to peel off his white duck coat and hold it out the next time the snake lunged; he then threw himself onto the coat and snake and "screamed like a lunatic." Eventually, a terrified Chinese boy came to his assistance, and together they twisted the coat around the snake's head and removed the serpent to its new quarters.

What a snake! What a tale! No wonder king cobras are featured attractions at zoos around the world. And no wonder I felt nervous when the Nashville Zoo's curator of reptiles removed a king cobra from her cage for John Netherton to photograph, while I stood only a few feet behind.

I recalled Gadow's description of the king, published in 1901—"its size and very poisonous nature make it the curse of the jungle"—and remembered Buck's warning: "Nowhere in the world is there an animal or reptile that can quite match its unfailing determination to wipe out anything that crosses its path. This lust to kill invests the king cobra with a quality of fiendishness that puts it in a class by itself, almost making of it a jungle synonym for death."

But the king cobra before us somehow lacked that air of fiendishness. Nowhere near the world's record of 18 feet 4 inches (5.58 m), this shorter serpent, like its smaller Asiatic cobra relatives, didn't even have much of a hood. It was rather drab looking, too: olive gray, with light crossbands.

Curiously, it seemed to like being held by Dale McGinnity, the curator, although once it was placed on a table it immediately began to investigate its surroundings. Intrigued by John's lighting stands, it tried to coil its body around some of his equipment; later, it wrapped itself around one leg of the table. It also showed an interest in some nearby gecko cages.

The king cobra is the only known snake species that constructs a nest for egg incubation.

125

"The serpent has many and more impressive qualities. First and foremost is the strength and lastingness of the impression produced by its strangeness, and its beautiful, infinitely varied, and, to the unscientific mind, causeless motions; its spectre-like silence and subtlety; its infinite patience and watchfulness, and its power to continue with raised head and neck rigid . . . ; and its wonderful quietude . . . lying as if in a deep perpetual sleep, yet eternally awake, with open brilliant eyes fixed on whosoever regards it. A sense of mystery becomes inseparably associated with its appearance."
—W. H. Hudson,
The Book of a Naturalist, 1919

King cobra

The world's largest venomous snake, the king cobra is agile and excitable and can inject a staggering quantity of venom into its victims. King cobras defend themselves readily, hissing or growling like a dog and moving forward while maintaining the hooded threat posture.

126

Perhaps this snake was manifesting the celebrated "curiosity" or "intelligence" attributed to its species by many herpetologists. Richardson asserts that "everybody who has had anything to do with hamadryads [king cobras] will tell you they are the most intelligent of all snakes." Ditmars says individuals learn to detect the character of glass and avoid bumping their noses, and some appear to recognize their handlers, coming to the door of a cage, peering up or down, and watching for their keeper, while reacting antagonistically toward strangers.

But these serpents are dangerous, too. The longest venomous snake in the world, the king cobra is a threat not only because of its body size and "insolent" disposition, but also because of its enormous venom glands. This cobra can inject "a staggering amount of venom," says Richard Conniff, who surveyed leading authorities on animal toxins to determine the world's ten most venomous creatures. In fact, king cobras in Thailand have reportedly killed work elephants after biting them where the toenail meets the skin of the foot. King cobras have a penchant for hanging on and chewing, extending the period of envenomation; a cobra that bit a tea picker in India retained its grip on her leg for eight minutes. She died twenty minutes after being bitten.

King cobras generally live in forests some distance from villages and cities in their native Asia, where their range extends from India through Vietnam into southern China and the Philippines; many bites are reported each year, however, perhaps because sandals worn by natives are less protective than high-top boots.

The king cobra is the only known snake species that constructs a nest for egg incubation. First, the female loops her body around bamboo leaves and other decaying vegetation and drags the decaying vegetation to the nest site with her coils. Then she hollows out two chambers in her pile of debris: one below, for the eggs, and one above, where she remains to guard the eggs. The male cobra customarily remains nearby. The female probably provides some warmth during the incubation process, though decomposing plant matter gives off heat as well. Her eighteen to forty-three eggs hatch two to three months later.

Cobras guarding their nests can be more dangerous than those encountered during other seasons of the year. An angered king cobra stretches the skin across its neck ribs into a hood, sways the upper part of its body, and makes a hissing sound that sounds like the growl of a small dog. According to Hans-Gunther Petzold, this is the only cobra that can move its body forward while maintaining the threat posture.

The king cobra preys chiefly on nonvenomous snakes, including pythons, but will consume venomous kraits on occasion. In captivity they have been known to resort to cannibalism.

As for that king cobra at the Nashville Zoo, did it hiss at its handler, spook photographer John Netherton with its threat posture, and strike menacingly at the author of this book?

No.

In fact, it flared its hood only *after* it was returned safely to its exhibition area, where it turned back, out of curiosity, to observe us through the feeding door.

"Sorry," McGinnity apologized afterward, perhaps embarrassed that his king cobra had showed no inclination to sink its jaws into our flesh or flaunt its legendary aggressiveness. "She's just so damn sweet."

An angered king cobra stretches the skin across its neck ribs into a hood, sways the upper part of its body, and makes a hissing sound often compared to the growl of a small dog.

Chapter 4

Snake Conservation

"The decline of snakes in our changing world has gone on unmonitored. Others have spoken for cranes and whales, and I hasten to say these words in praise of snakes, whose silent spring is also far along."
—Archie Carr,
"In Praise of Snakes," 1971

Rough green snake
Facing page: *The greatest threat to snakes is man. Pesticides are responsible for killing many insect-eating green snakes and other harmless species in gardens, and lawn mowers and automobiles also take a heavy toll.*

Rainbow boa
Inset: *Boas and pythons around the world are protected by the Convention on International Trade in Endangered Species of Wild Fauna and Flora (CITES) treaty. Reptile smuggling is a "high-profit criminal enterprise," says U.S. Fish and Wildlife Service Director Jamie Rappaport Clark, "and the United States is its largest market."*

"Snakes are probably disappearing at a more rapidly rising rate than any other group of vertebrates," herpetologist Archie Carr warned thirty-five years ago.

Unfortunately, no one was listening.

Carr's concerns have an especially chilling effect today, in light of recent evidence of declines in amphibian populations around the world.

Reflecting on Rachel Carson's shocking best seller *Silent Spring*, Carr noted that "the silence she had in mind was lost birdsong on a poisoned earth"—but, he added, "snakes are harder to find than birds. Because [their] ways are secret, the decline of snakes in our changing world has gone on almost unmonitored. Others have spoken for cranes and whales, and I hasten to say these words in praise of snakes, whose silent spring is also far along."

Too far along to dismiss, yet so imperfectly documented as to make it difficult to convince others—particularly those who detest snakes.

Why is there so little empirical evidence to support Carr's claim of declines in snake populations? First, without question, because snakes lead secretive lives and are difficult to find. Scientists have enough trouble trying to census populations of frogs, whose males at least *sing* in the spring and summer, signaling which species are in the neighborhood. Moreover, many male frogs are considerate enough to assemble in large choruses to announce their availability and readiness to mate with nearby females—which makes the counting process easier.

Threats to snakes are everywhere: destruction of habitat, the result of urban expansion and commercial development, highway construction, drainage of swamps and wetlands, logging, burning and bulldozing of rain forests, elimination of floodplains, damming of rivers and streams, and overgrazing of grasslands.

Snakes, on the other hand, do not sing—they lack the requisite vocal cords with which to serenade the opposite sex. So unless field biologists happen upon a swarm of garter snakes, an aggregation of anacondas, a cluster of carpet pythons, or a bola of rattlesnakes, they may have little idea whether snake populations inhabit a given locale.

True, the introduction of radiotelemetry in recent years has made it possible to monitor the whereabouts and movements of individual snakes, but only those that can first be caught and implanted. Counting, or even estimating, the number of individuals in a population poses nearly insurmountable challenges.

Even if a reliable system for counting snakes did exist—generating data to compare population sizes over time and to confirm anecdotal reports of dwindling snake numbers—the next hurdles would be obtaining adequate funding for fieldwork and implementing conservation strategies.

"People love the hot and furries," says Michael Bruton, director of the Educational Trust of the Two Oceans Aquarium, "but they don't like conserving the wet and slimies. Anyone who has tried to raise money for frog or snake or eel conservation, or fish conservation, or insect conservation, has a heck of a job, compared to the fabulous fur balls."

In one of the most significant studies of the population biology of a reptile species, Louis Guillette of the University of Florida discovered that a chemical spill at a Florida pesticide plant seriously affected alligators in nearby Lake Apopka. Guillette and his colleagues found increased mortality rates among baby gators, lower sperm counts and smaller penis size among adult males, structural defects in testicles, and abnormalities in female ovaries. Publication of their findings attracted the attention of some mainstream media, but Guillette concedes that no one offered to fund a study of the effect of the chemical spill on water snakes at the same lake.

"Observations of pesticide effects on amphibians and reptiles are usually made casually in the course of other studies," Robert Rudd noted more than thirty years ago. "Hence there is not a large body of data on which to base conclusions." Isolated reports of mortality exist, but scientific evidence of reptile or snake sensitivity to pesticides and other chemicals is rare.

Still, the evidence of worldwide declines in amphibian populations should serve as an early warning signal to biologists and the public that snakes are in jeopardy, too. The reduction in frog populations alone, argues Richard Shine, "may be a catastrophe for the snakes," since many snakes depend upon frogs as their principal source of food.

Threats to snakes are omnipresent—they can be found everywhere you look. Foremost among them is destruction of habitat, the result of urban expansion and commercial development, highway construction, drainage of swamps and wetlands, logging, burning and bulldozing of rain forests, elimination of floodplains, damming of rivers and streams, and overgrazing of grasslands.

Such disturbances of existing reptile habitats not only wipe out entire populations of snakes, they also cause fragmentation and isolation of survivors within their range. This, in turn, wreaks havoc on reproductive behavior, creating shortages of sexually mature mates (hence smaller breeding pools) and prompting genetic inbreeding, hybridization between species, and greater susceptibility to disease.

Equally devastating is the impact of pollution on wildlife, habitats, and entire ecosystems. The range of these pollutants is shocking: toxic chemicals and sewage from industries, municipalities, and households drain into natural water supplies or are buried where they contaminate the soil and leach into the watershed. Agricultural runoff carries pesticides, herbicides, fertilizers, and animal wastes into waterways, disturbing aquatic ecosystems and adding to the contamination of the water supply. Emissions from smokestacks and automobiles contribute to acid rain and acid snow. These pollutants significantly impact the land, water, and vegetation where snakes live and breed, poisoning juvenile and adult snakes along with other wildlife on which they depend. Especially troubling are contaminants such as mercury, heavy metals, and oxides, which reach the water supply and accumulate in the aquatic food web.

"The effects of these pollutants on snakes have been little studied, but they almost certainly do have a significant impact," says herpetologist John A. Burton. "Snakes are predators, and many are near the top of a food chain . . . feeding on lizards and small mammals, which in turn prey on the insects that are likely to be poisoned. The pesticides build up in animals along the food chain and become concentrated, so they have the most effect on top predators."

And there's more. Climate change and natural catastrophes—including drought, floods, hurricanes, typhoons, earthquakes, forest fires, heat waves, and global warming—also claim a heavy toll on the world's herpetofauna. Parasite infestations and diseases are another concern; currently, many scientists believe that the extinction of certain species of frogs and recent die-offs of frog populations in Central America and elsewhere are caused by an unknown fungus or protozoan. Introduction of non-native ("exotic") species of wildlife, which prey directly on snakes or compete for the same foods, is disruptive, too. And increased levels of ultraviolet-B radiation, the result of thinning of the atmosphere's protective ozone layer, have been found responsible for high mortality among frog eggs and larvae and for deformities in salamanders.

The greatest threat to snakes, it is obvious, is man. Man routinely butchers snakes on sight; crushes them beneath his tires; pours gasoline down their holes and pumps auto exhaust fumes into their dens; strips off their skins to make belts and boots; chops off their heads to encase in paperweights; stuffs their bodies in gro-

Red-shouldered hawk eating snake
Wildlife refuges and national parks are designed to encourage and preserve species diversity. In Everglades National Park, a red-shouldered hawk eats a snake, which itself preyed on green tree frogs and small fish. When nonnative species—for example, the Cuban tree frog, which is currently decimating Everglades green tree frog populations—are introduced to an ecosystem by humans, the balance of nature is upset.

Some two hundred species of snakes worldwide are threatened or endangered.

tesque poses for the curio trade; melts down their fat for liniments and "health" products; eats their flesh and drinks their blood in restaurants; milks and sells their venom; collects their carcasses for bounties; and snatches them in the wild—legally and illegally—for the burgeoning pet trade.

More than half a century ago, Clifford H. Pope estimated that "nearly six million snakes must be mashed out of existence every twelve months." Today the figure is probably even higher. Steve Grenard calculates that more than half a million rattlesnakes alone are killed each year for rattlesnake roundups in Texas, Oklahoma, Pennsylvania, and Georgia. The true extent of the slaughter of serpents worldwide, of course, cannot be measured.

The time has come for humans to get over their irrational fear of snakes and start thinking about the bigger picture. Kill off the snakes—the nonvenomous ones along with the venomous—and the world's rodent populations will explode. Rats. Mice. These and other vermin that carry fleas and ticks, which in turn harbor viruses that can trigger fatal diseases, even plagues.

"If we lose the snakes," Shine concludes, "the consequences for other animals are likely to be profound."

Around the world, environmental groups and concerned citizens are fighting to preserve threatened and endangered species of wildlife, especially such "charismatic megafauna" as pandas, tigers, whales, and elephants. For snakes to be accorded similar prominence, however, would be unheard of.

Nonetheless, some two hundred species of snakes worldwide are threatened or endangered, according to Harry Greene. In North America, the San Francisco garter snake, giant garter snake, Eastern indigo snake, Concho water snake, copperbelly water snake, Atlantic salt marsh snake, Alameda whipsnake, New Mexico ridge-nosed rattlesnake, Puerto Rican boa, Mona boa, and Virgin Islands tree boa are all listed as threatened or endangered under the Endangered Species Act. Worldwide, even more species are threatened or endangered. All boas and pythons, and a number of other snakes, are protected by the Convention on International Trade in Endangered Species of Wild Fauna and Flora (CITES) treaty, which regulates or restricts export.

But international treaties, federal regulations, state laws, and local ordinances cannot, by themselves, prevent unscrupulous and irresponsible individuals from exploiting and exterminating snakes. Astonishingly, illegal trade in animals is the second-largest black market activity after drugs, according to the U.S. Fish and Wildlife Service.

Clearly, there is little hope of preventing a "silent spring" for snakes unless political and environmental leaders, law enforcement officials, educators, scientists, and citizens become more active guardians of our natural resources, including herpetofauna. The acquisition and protection of habitats and ecosystems, which are essential to maintaining biological diversity, should be higher on the nation's list of priorities, backed up by more aggressive enforcement of environmental statutes and international trade laws.

Shine and other herpetologists agree that the key to changing entrenched negative attitudes about snakes is education: "We need to teach our children to conserve ecosystems and species," he says. Adds Howard K. Reinert: "Protection and maintenance of suitable habitat are of paramount importance for long-term survival of wild snake species."

Why bother? ask some members of society. If the vital role of snakes in controlling rodent pests—consuming tons of rats and mice every year—doesn't sound compelling enough, then perhaps the direct medical benefits to mankind might carry some weight. Snake venoms have already been used, or are currently being experimented with, for treatment of cancer, heart disease, hypertension, nerve diseases, epilepsy, leukemia, and immotile sperm. According to Grenard, cobra venom is widely used for the relief of pain in cancer patients, as well as for migraine, syphilis, and spinal afflictions. The venom of the Russell's viper has been used clinically for treatment of hemophilia; venom of the saw-scaled viper can prevent bone loss, or osteoporosis; and venom of the Malayan pit viper is of medical value for blood clotting and treatment of sickle cell anemia.

"Snake venom," F. Harvey Pough et al. pointed out in 1998, "is one of the most expensive natural resources on Earth. Depending on the species, venom is worth 5 to 1,000 times as much as gold!"

The variety of species in nature—venomous and nonvenomous snakes included—can be compared to a "vast library of unread books," writes conservationist Peter Matthiessen, "and the plundering of nature is comparable to the random discarding of whole volumes without having opened them and learned from them." Indifference to species loss, he concludes, is "indifference to the future, and therefore a shameful carelessness about our children."

Long before Benjamin Franklin made his case for the timber rattlesnake as the symbol of our new nation, this serpent had already been brandished on colonial flags, where it coiled fearlessly above the slogan Don't Tread on Me. Two and a quarter centuries later, that admonition remains sound. As civilization continues to encroach on the domain of this snake and others, we must work harder to heed that warning. If we do not, the day may dawn when there are none left to tread on at all.

Hog-nosed snake victim

Snake mortality rates are especially high on roadways, since snakes often seek out the heat of sun-warmed asphalt to raise their body temperature on a cold night. Many drivers cruelly swerve out of their way to kill harmless snakes because of an irrational hatred of serpents.

Snake Photography

Snake photography, John Netherton has said, is even more challenging than frog photography.

Naturally, I assumed he meant that the speed of his subjects—and the risk associated with photographing venomous species—posed the challenge. During our previous collaboration on a book about frogs, I had marveled at John's patience in dealing with the slippery, long-legged creatures: all too often, they just wouldn't sit still. This time around, his subjects not only moved with the speed of lightning, some were also inclined to bite.

Over time, however, I realized John meant something else. He was concerned, he said, with taking photographs that would give a distinct look to his subjects. "Many photographers depict snakes doing what comes naturally: lying outstretched, flat on the ground," John explained. "It was obvious I'd have to come up with some more interesting ways to photograph my subjects. After I examined the photographs of snakes in field guides and other volumes, I sensed this would be my hardest assignment."

Two-striped forest pit viper
Facing page: *The light green coloration of the two-striped forest pit viper, or Amazonian palm viper, offers excellent camouflage when this snake seeks shelter in palms and other trees. Adults retain a distinctive russet color on their tail, a characteristic more common to juveniles of other species.*

Green cat-eyed snake
Inset: *To photograph a green cat-eyed snake, an Asian rear-fanged species that envenomates its prey by chewing, photographer John Netherton used longer lenses for safety purposes and to avoid harassing the snake.*

For a while, John seemed to favor head shots—sharp-focus pictures that revealed the full splendor of the eye, the beguiling curve of the mouth, the unusual pits on a pit viper or a python, and the enticing tongue. I especially liked his tongue shots, until he pointed out they all looked alike.

"What do you think we should call the book?" John joked one day. *"The Book of Tongues?"*

He had a point.

Having already made fun of my affinity for "friendly" snakes (I had argued that photos of too many scary-looking specimens might spook the very readers who needed to see that not all snakes are intimidating), John was clearly evolving his own notions of what constituted viable images.

Using Nikon F5 and N90S cameras and various lenses (including the Nikkor 200mm micro, 70–180mm micro, and a 20–35mm lens for desert work), John experimented with the range of lighting, utilizing his Nikon SB-26 and SB-28 Speedlights, and SB-21 Macro Speedlight.

"I like to position one flash to light the snake frontally, and a second flash either for backlighting or sidelighting," John explains. "These little nuances can turn an otherwise flat-looking image into a far more pleasing photograph."

Backgrounds, too, were a major concern.

"I can't emphasize enough how important backgrounds are," he says. "A beautiful milk snake crawling in a clump of grass or lying flat on a rock might be fine for identification shots, but aesthetically it just doesn't work. And keep in mind, too much clutter distracts from the snake."

While John was preoccupied with composition, lighting, film stock (Kodak Lumiere X), and other particulars, I was mostly worried he might get bitten.

Fortunately, before leaving Tennessee to photograph rattlesnakes in Arizona, he made arrangements with a friend at Nikon to provide an experimental video contraption hooked up to a still camera. ("We moved the still camera in while watching the snake on a video monitor," John relates.

"The camera was mounted on a monopod—like a pole. I wanted to be able to show the background and the cactus while the black-tailed rattler remained in the foreground.")

For the most part, taking pictures of rattlesnakes in the desert proved less stressful than working under controlled conditions at some zoos.

"In Florida, I was working with a herpetologist at a zoo, and the monocled cobra kept chasing us. The herpetologist had to keep grabbing it and pulling it back to where I wanted to photograph it. I was outside, low on the ground, and trying to get the sky in the picture.

"Another time, we had a rattlesnake on an enclosed grassy area at a zoo, and I got bitten. But not by the snake. I was down on the ground and apparently rolled across a nest of fire ants. There I was, knocking them off—feeling a burning pain."

While in Florida, John visited herpetologist Bill Haast, internationally acclaimed for his pioneering work with venomous snakes, which he milks for research labs to produce antivenom serums for hospitals.

John was astonished by Haast's dexterity with serpents.

"They roll in this metal cart with thrashing cobras and mambas—the snakes understand they're about to be milked and fed—and he opens it, and they flare up. Bill holds out one hand to get their attention and grabs them and then takes them to an area in his laboratory to extract the venom." (Two decades earlier, I had met Haast when he was director of the Miami Serpentarium. Then, as now, he would regularly inject himself with diluted venoms to build up conditional immunity to the occasional bites he endures while handling dangerous snakes.)

In June 1997, midway through the photography for this book, John was preparing to drive to Reelfoot Lake in West Tennessee when he suddenly felt chest pains. He turned his van around and headed instead to a medical clinic, where he was diagnosed as having just suffered a heart attack. Within an hour, he was in a Nashville hospital undergoing an emergency angioplasty procedure for a blocked artery. When he was released a few days later, his cardiologist advised him to take it easy.

Whereupon John—perhaps newly energized by the surge of blood coursing through his reopened artery—immediately rescheduled a photo shoot at the Nashville Zoo that had been canceled while he was in the hospital. Then, on what turned out to be one of the hottest days of the year, we took off early for a day at the zoo.

"Actually, I knew that surgery was still a possibility," John later admitted, "and I expected the doctor might ground me. That's why I wanted to get those pictures."

It proved to be quite a day. Ensconced in a back room where the herpetology staff houses specimens not currently on exhibit in the Reptile House, John set up his camera equipment and light stands and began photographing venomous snakes provided by curator Dale McGinnity. Unfortunately, a raccoon had sabotaged the room's air-conditioning system the night before, and everyone—especially John—began sweating profusely. (Later I learned that John's excessive sweating might not have been caused solely by the room's infernal temperatures. But that was after his cardiologist announced bypass surgery was necessary.)

Meanwhile, three ravishing eyelash vipers, one enormous king cobra, several handsome Carolina pigmy rattlesnakes, and a few other specimens were carefully lifted out of their display cages for John to photograph. (I hovered a few feet behind John, nervous as always, but at the same time oddly exhilarated that we could stand so close to these deadly creatures without feeling any immediate threat.)

And John got some spectacular photographs. From time to time, we would drag him out of the room for a blast of air-conditioning, and on these occasions he would set up his lights and take pictures of other venomous serpents behind glass.

The green mamba ("just too dangerous to work with," according to McGinnity) also had to be shot from behind glass. "I used two flashes positioned off to each side and a black poster board to eliminate reflections in the glass," John explains. "I cut a hole in the center of the board where the lens protruded and used the adapter ring that holds the SB-21 Macro Speedlight to hold the poster board in place."

One week later, after undergoing heart bypass surgery, John remained pleased that the zoo shoot had gone so well and that he now had those photographs under his belt.

But under his shirt he also had a hole in his chest, and it took him longer to recover than anticipated. When his cardiologist finally said he could lift objects over five pounds (e.g., his camera) and resume work, I offered him an appropriately low-key subject: a pair of worm snakes. Other specimens were to follow, including—at long last—a green snake.

Green snakes had been the subject of ongoing discussion for months. I had hinted I wouldn't write the text unless John photographed one, but the only green snakes he had managed to locate had been run over by traffic.

Then Brian Miller, a colleague at Middle Tennessee State University, saved the day: encountering a beautiful green snake sunning itself on a road, he leaped from his car, caught the snake, and brought it to school for me to pass along to John. But that evening, after John drove to Franklin to fetch the snake, his van broke down; the only way to get the snake back to his studio in West Nashville, he concluded, would be by taxi. Sometime after 11 p.m., he finally stepped into a cab—the green snake tucked discreetly out of sight.

John enjoys recounting this and other anecdotes about his photography for this volume—tangling with a cantankerous hog-nosed snake, chasing in the dark after a water snake that was pursuing a hapless toad, and watching the telltale eyes of a copperhead shift ever so slightly as he set up a shot. Yet, in the end, he feels there is something far more important to communicate.

"I believe I have a responsibility to capture on film the varied behaviors that will convince people that snakes aren't the villains they're portrayed as in films like *Anaconda*," John declares. "For thousands of years, the serpent has had a stigma attached to it. That stigma isn't deserved.

"Snakes are as varied in behavior, color, shape, and size as any other group of animals. And many are far more interesting."

Bibliography

Adams, Douglas, and Mark Carwardine. *Last Chance to See.* New York: Harmony Books, 1990.

Appleby, Leonard. "Snakes Shedding Skin." *Natural History,* 89:2 (February 1980): pp. 64–71.

Aymar, Brandt, ed. *Treasury of Snake Lore.* New York: Greenberg Publisher, 1956.

Barbour, Roger W. *Amphibians & Reptiles of Kentucky.* Lexington: University Press of Kentucky, 1971.

Bartram, William. *Travels of William Bartram,* ed. by Mark Van Doren. New York: Dover Publications, 1955. Originally published 1928.

Bauchot, Roland, ed. *Snakes: A Natural History.* New York: Sterling Publishing Co., 1994.

Bechtel, H. Bernard. *Reptile and Amphibian Variants: Colors, Patterns, and Scales.* Malabar, FL: Krieger Publishing Co., 1995.

Bellairs, Angus, and Carrington, Richard. *The World of Reptiles.* New York: American Elsevier Publishing Co., 1966.

Bogert, Charles M. *The Animal Kingdom, Vol. II, Book III: Amphibians and Reptiles of the World.* New York: Greystone Press, 1954, pp. 1189–1390.

Brazaitis, Peter, and Watanabe, Myrna E. *The World of Snakes.* Blacksburg, VA: Tetra Press, 1993.

Breckenridge, W. J. *Reptiles and Amphibians of Minnesota.* Minneapolis: University of Minnesota Press, 1944.

Buck, Frank, with Edward Anthony. *Bring 'Em Back Alive.* New York: Simon and Schuster, 1930.

Burton, John A. *The Book of Snakes.* New York: Crescent Books, 1991.

Caldwell, Michael W., and Michael S. Y. Lee. "A Snake with Legs From the Marine Cretaceous of the Middle East." *Nature,* 386:6626 (April 17, 1997): pp. 705–709.

Campbell, Jonathan A., and William W. Lamar. *The Venomous Reptiles of Latin America.* Ithaca, NY: Comstock Publishing Associates, 1989.

Caras, Roger A. *Dangerous to Man,* revised ed. New York: Holt, Rinehart and Winston, 1975.

Carmichael, Pete, and Williams, Winston. *Florida's Fabulous Reptiles and Amphibians.* Tampa, FL: World Publications, 1991.

Carr, Archie. *The Reptiles.* New York: Time-Life Books, 1963.

Carr, Archie. *A Naturalist in Florida: A Celebration of Eden,* edited by Marjorie Harris Carr. New Haven, CT: Yale University Press, 1994.

Cloudsley-Thompson, J. L. *Predation and Defence Amongst Reptiles.* Bristol: Longdunn Press, Ltd., 1994.

Collins, Joseph T. *Amphibians and Reptiles in Kansas.* Lawrence: University of Kansas Publications, 1974.

Conant, Roger, and Joseph T. Collins. *A Field Guide to Reptiles and Amphibians: Eastern and Central North America.* 3rd ed. Peterson Field Guide Series. Boston: Houghton Mifflin, 1991.

Conniff, Richard. "The Ten Most Venomous Animals." *International Wildlife,* 18:2 (March-April, 1988): pp. 18–25.

Cook, Patrick M., Matthew P. Rowe, and R. Wayne Van Devender. "Allometric Scaling and Interspecific Differences in the Rattling Sounds of Rattlesnakes." *Herpetologica,* 50:3 (September 1994): pp. 358–68.

Costanzo, Jon P. "Recovery From Ice-Entombment in Garter Snakes." *Herpetological Review,* 19:4 (December 1988): pp. 76–77.

Covington, Dennis. *Salvation on Sand Mountain: Snake Handling and Redemption in Southern Appalachia.* NY: Penguin, 1995.

Crompton, John. *Snake Lore.* Garden City, NY: Doubleday & Company, 1964.

Devine, Michael C. "Copulatory Plugs, Restricted Mating Opportunities and Reproductive Competition Among Male Garter Snakes." *Nature,* 267:5609 (May 26, 1977): pp. 345–46.

Ditmars, Raymond L. *Snakes of the World.* New York: Pyramid Publications, 1962. Originally published 1931.

Ditmars, Raymond L. *Confessions of a Scientist.* New York: Books for Libraries Press, 1970. Originally published 1934.

Ditmars, Raymond L. *The Reptiles of North America.* New York: Doubleday & Co., 1936.

Dobie, J. Frank. *Rattlesnakes.* Austin: University of Texas Press, 1965.

Dodd, C. Kenneth, Jr. "Strategies for Snake Conservation." In *Snakes: Ecology and Behavior,* ed. by Richard Seigel and Joseph T. Collins. New York: McGraw Hill, 1993, pp. 363–393.

Ernst, Carl H. *Venomous Reptiles of North America.* Washington, D.C.: Smithsonian Institution Press, 1992.

Ernst, Carl H., and Roger W. Barbour. *Snakes of Eastern North America.* Fairfax, VA: George Mason University Press, 1989.

Ernst, Carl H., and George R. Zug. *Snakes in Question.* Washington, D.C.: Smithsonian Institution Press, 1996.

Fitch, Henry S. *A Demographic Study of the Ringneck Snake* (Diadophis punctatus) *in Kansas.* Lawrence, KS: University of Kansas Museum of Natural History, Miscellaneous Publications no. 62, April 3, 1975.

Ford, Neil B. "Experimental Design in Studies of Snake Behavior." *Herpetological Monographs,* no. 9 (1995): pp. 130–139.

Franklin, Benjamin. "The Rattle-Snake as a Symbol of America." *Writings,* ed. by J. A. Leo Lemay. New York: Library of America, 1987, pp. 744–747. Originally published 1775.

Franklin, Benjamin. "The Turk'y Is In Comparison a Much More Respectable Bird." *Writings,* ed. by J. A. Leo Lemay. New York: Library of America, 1987, pp: 1084–1089. Letter dated Jan. 26, 1784.

Freud, Sigmund. *The Interpretation of Dreams.* New York: Avon Books, 1965.

Gadow, Hans. *The Cambridge Natural History: Amphibia and Reptiles.* Vol. 8. Codicote, England: Wheldon & Wesley, Ltd., 1958. Originally published 1901.

Gaulden, Robert L. "Tiger by the Trail." *Reptiles*, 5:9 (September 1997), pp. 10–18.

Gloyd, Howard K., and Roger Conant. *Snakes of the Agkistrodon Complex: A Monographic Review*. Oxford, OH: Society for the Study of Amphibians and Reptiles, 1990.

Godey, John. *The Snake*. New York: G. P. Putnam's Sons, 1978.

Greene, Harry W. *Snakes: The Evolution of Mystery in Nature*. Photographs by Michael and Patricia Fogden. Berkeley: University of California Press, 1997.

Greene, Harry W., and Jonathan A. Campbell. "The Future of Pitvipers," in *Biology of the Pitvipers*, ed. by Jonathan A. Campbell and Edmund D. Brodie, Jr. Tyler, TX: Selva, 1992, pp. 421–427.

Greene, Harry W., and Roy McDiarmid. "Coral Snake Mimicry: Does It Occur?" *Science*, 213 (1981): pp. 1207–1212.

Grenard, Steve. *Medical Herpetology*. Pottsville, PA: N G Publishing Inc., 1994.

Grzimek, Bernhard, ed. *Grzimek's Animal Life Encyclopedia*, Vol. 6, *Reptiles*. New York: Van Nostrand Reinhold Co., 1975.

Guillette, Louis J., Jr., D. B. Pickford, D. A. Crain, A. A. Rooney, and H. F. Percival. "Reduction in Penis Size and Plasma Testosterone Concentrations in Juvenile Alligators Living in a Contaminated Environment." *General and Comparative Endicrinology*, 101 (1996): pp. 32–42.

Hardy, David L., Sr. "A Re-evaluation of Suffocation as the Cause of Death During Constriction By Snakes." *Herpetological Review* (March 1994), 25:2, pp. 45–47.

Henderson, Robert W., and Mary H. Binder. *The Ecology and Behavior of Vine Snakes (Ahaetulla, Oxybelis, Thelotornis, Uromacer): A Review*. Contributions in Biology and Geology, no. 37. Milwaukee, WI: Milwaukee Public Museum, 1980.

Herszenhorn, David. "13-Foot Pet Python Kills Its Caretaker." *The New York Times*, Oct. 10, 1996.

Heuvelmans, Bernard. *On the Track of Unknown Animals*. New York: Hill and Wang, 1959.

Holmes, Oliver Wendell. *Elsie Venner: A Romance of Destiny*. New York: New York Publishing Co., 1861.

Hoser, Raymond T. "Australian Pythons (Part 1): Genera *Chondropython* and *Aspidites*." *The Herptile*, 6:2 (June 1981): pp. 10–16.

Hoser, Raymond T. *Australian Reptiles & Frogs*. Sydney, Australia: Pierson & Co., 1989.

Howey, J. Oldfield. *The Encircled Serpent: A Study of Serpent Symbolism in All Countries and Ages*. New York: Arthur Richmond Co., 1955.

Hudson, W. H. *The Naturalist in La Plata*. New York: E. P. Dutton, 1892.

Hudson, W. H. *The Book of a Naturalist*. New York: E. P. Dutton, 1919.

Isemonger, Richard M. *Snakes of Africa: Southern, Central and East*. New York: Thomas Nelson & Sons, 1962.

Jackson, Jerome A. "Gray Rat Snakes Versus Red-Cockaded Woodpeckers: Predator-Prey Adaptations." *The Auk*, 91:2 (April 1974): pp. 342–347.

Kardong, Kenneth V. *Vertebrates: Comparative Anatomy, Function, Evolution*. 2nd edition. Boston, WCB McGraw-Hill, 1998.

Kauffeld, Carl. *Snakes and Snake Hunting*. Malabar, FL: Krieger Publishing Co., 1995. Originally published 1957.

Kauffeld, Carl. *Snakes: The Keeper and the Kept*. New York: Doubleday & Co., 1969.

Klauber, Laurence M. *Rattlesnakes: Their Habits, Life Histories, & Influence on Mankind*. Abridged edition. Berkeley: University of California Press, 1982. Originally published 1956.

La Barre, Weston. *They Shall Take Up Serpents: Psychology of the Southern Snake-Handling Cult*. New York: Schocken Books, 1969.

Lewis, Meriwether. *The Journals of the Lewis & Clark Expedition*, ed. by Gary E. Moulton. Vol. 3. Lincoln: University of Nebraska Press, 1987.

Lillywhite, Harvey B. "Snakes Under Pressure." *Natural History*, 96:11 (November 1987): pp. 58–67.

Lipske, Michael. "Sex and the Single Garter Snake." *Wildlife Conservation*, 100:4 (July/August 1997), pp. 44–51.

Maitland, D. P. "Scaling Trees." *New Scientist* (on-line) "Last Word Archive," Sept. 18, 1997.

Mason, Robert T., and David Crews. "Female Mimicry in Garter Snakes." *Nature*, 316:6023 (July 4, 1985): pp. 59–60.

Mason, Robert T., et al. "Sex Pheromones in Snakes." *Science*, 245:4915 (July 21, 1989): pp. 290–293.

Matthiessen, Peter. *Wildlife in America*, revised edit. New York: Viking, 1987.

Mattison, Chris. *Snakes of the World*. New York: Facts on File, 1986.

Mattison, Chris. *The Encyclopedia of Snakes*. New York: Facts on File, 1995.

Mattison, Chris. *Rattler! A Natural History of Rattlesnakes*. London: Blandford, 1996.

May, Peter G., et al. "Seasonal Abundance and Activity of a Rattlesnake (*Sistrurus miliarius barbouri*) in Central Florida." *Copeia*, no. 2 (May 16, 1996): pp. 389–401.

May, Peter G., Steven T. Heulett, Terence M. Farrell, and Melissa A. Pilgrim. "Live Fast, Love Hard, and Die Young: The Ecology of Pigmy Rattlesnakes." *Reptile & Amphibian Magazine*, no. 45 (January/February 1997): pp. 36–49.

Mehrtens, John M. *Living Snakes of the World in Color*. New York: Sterling, 1987.

Merker, Gerold, and Cindy Merker. "The Mystical Gray-Banded: Gem of the North American Kingsnakes." *Reptiles*, 4:7 (July 1996): pp. 60–85.

Mertens, Robert. *The World of Amphibians and Reptiles*. New York: McGraw-Hill, 1960.

Minton, Sherman A., and Madge Rutherford Minton. *Venomous Reptiles*. New York: Scribner's, 1969.

Minton, Sherman A., and Madge Rutherford Minton. *Giant Reptiles*. New York: Scribner's, 1973.

Mitchell, Joseph C. *The Reptiles of Virginia*. Washington, D.C.: Smithsonian Institution Press, 1994.

Morgan, Ann H. *Kinships of Animals and Man: A Textbook of Animal Biology*. New York: McGraw-Hill, 1955.

Morris, Percy A. *An Introduction to the Reptiles and Amphibians of the United States*. (Formerly titled *They Hop and They Crawl*.) New York: Dover Publications, 1974. Originally published 1944.

Morris, Ramona, and Desmond Morris. *Men and Snakes*. New York: McGraw-Hill, 1965.

Muir, John. *The Story of My Boyhood and Youth*. Madison: University of Wisconsin Press, 1965. Originally published 1916.

Muir, John. *A Thousand-Mile Walk to the Gulf*. San Francisco: Sierra Club Books, 1991. Originally published 1916.

Nichol, John. *Bites & Stings: The World of Venomous Animals*. New York: Facts on

File, 1989.

Nissenson, Marilyn, and Susan Jonas. *Snake Charm*. New York: Harry N. Abrams, 1995.

Noss, Reed F. "The Naturalists Are Dying Off." *Journal of Conservation Biology*, 10:1 (February 1996): pp. 1–3.

Obst, Fritz J., Klaus Richter, and Udo Jacob. *The Completely Illustrated Atlas of Reptiles and Amphibians for the Terrarium*. Neptune City, NJ: T.F.H. Publications, 1988.

Palmer, Thomas. *Landscape with Reptile: Rattlesnakes in an Urban World*. New York: Ticknor & Fields, 1992.

Palmer, William M., and Alvin L. Braswell. *Reptiles of North Carolina*. Chapel Hill: University of North Carolina Press, 1995.

Panter-Downes, Mollie. "A Reporter At Large: Okapis, Herons, Bush Babies, and Blitzes." *The New Yorker* (March 7, 1942): pp. 36–44.

Petzold, Hans-Gunther. "Cobras," "Pit Vipers," and "Vipers," in *Grzimek's Animal Life Encyclopedia*, vol. 6, *Reptiles*. New York: Van Nostrand Reinhold Co., pp. 415–484.

Plummer, Michael V. "Nesting Movements, Nesting Behavior, and Nest Sites of Green Snakes (*Opheodrys aestivus*) Revealed by Radiotelemetry." *Herpetologica*, 46:2 (June, 1990), pp. 190–195.

Pope, Clifford H. *Snakes Alive and How They Live*. New York: Viking Press, 1937.

Pope, Clifford H. "A Python in the Home." *Chicago Natural History Museum Bulletin*. (April 1947): pp. 4–5.

Pope, Clifford H. *The Giant Snakes*. New York: Alfred A. Knopf, 1961.

Pough, F. Harvey, Rabin M. Andrews, John E. Cadle, Martha L. Crump, Alan H. Savitzky, and Kentwood D. Wells. *Herpetology*. Upper Saddle River, NJ: Prentice Hall, 1998.

Reinert, Howard K. "Radiotelemetric Field Studies of Pitvipers: Data Acquisition and Analysis." In *Biology of the Pitvipers*, ed. Jonathan A. Campbell and Edmund D. Brodie, Jr. Tyler, TX: Selva, 1992, pp. 185–197.

Reinert, Howard K. "Habit Selection in Snakes." In *Snakes: Ecology and Behavior*, Richard A. Seigel and Joseph T. Collins, eds. New York: McGraw Hill, 1993, pp. 201–240.

Richardson, Maurice. *The Fascination of Reptiles*. New York: Hill and Wang, 1972.

Roosevelt, Theodore. *A Book-Lover's Holidays in the Open*. New York: Charles Scribner's Sons, 1920.

Roosevelt, Theodore. *Theodore Roosevelt's Letters to His Children*, ed. by Joseph B. Bishop. New York: Charles Scribner's Sons, 1927.

Rossman, Douglas A., Neil B. Ford, and Richard A. Seigel. *The Garter Snakes: Evolution and Ecology*. Norman: University of Oklahoma Press, 1996.

Rudd, Robert L. *Pesticides and the Living Landscape*. Madison: University of Wisconsin Press, 1964.

Russell, Findlay E. *Snake Venom Poisoning*. Great Neck, NY: Scholium International Inc., 1983.

Saint-Girons, Hubert. "Physiology." In *Snakes: A Natural History*, Roland Bauchot, ed. New York: Sterling, 1995: pp. 76–91.

Schmidt, Karl P., and Robert F. Inger. *Living Reptiles of the World*. Garden City, NY: Hanover, 1957.

Schuett, Gordon W., et al. "Production of Offspring in the Absence of Males: Evidence for Facultative Parthenogenesis in Bisexual Snakes." *Herpetological Natural History*, 5:1 (June 1997): pp. 1–10.

Schweitzer, Albert. *The Animal World of Albert Schweitzer*. Translated and ed. by Charles R. Joy. Boston: Beacon Press, 1950.

Schwenk, Kurt. "Why Snakes Have Forked Tongues." *Science*, vol. 263 (March 18, 1994): pp. 1573–1577.

Schwenk, Kurt. "The Serpent's Tongue." *Natural History*, 104:4 (April 1995): pp. 48–55.

Seigel, Richard A., and Joseph T. Collins, eds. *Snakes: Ecology and Behavior*. New York: McGraw-Hill, 1993.

Shine, Richard. *Australian Snakes: A Natural History*. Ithaca, NY: Cornell University Press, 1991.

Simon, Hilda. *The Splendor of Iridescence: Structural Colors in the Animal Kingdom*. New York: Dodd, Mead & Company, 1971.

Slaughter, Thomas P. *The Natures of John and William Bartram*. New York: Knopf, 1996.

Smith, Malcolm A. *The British Amphibians & Reptiles*. London: Collins, 1969. Originally published 1951.

Staszko, Ray, and Jerry G. Walls. *Rat Snakes*. Neptune City, NJ: T.H.F. Publications, 1994.

Stebbins, Robert C. *Amphibians and Reptiles of Western North America*. New York: McGraw-Hill, 1954.

Stebbins, Robert C. *A Field Guide to Western Reptiles and Amphibians*. 2nd ed. Peterson Field Guide Series. Boston: Houghton Mifflin, 1985.

Stidworthy, John. *Snakes of the World*. New York: Bantam Books, 1972.

Tennant, Alan. *The Snakes of Texas*. Austin: Texas Monthly Press, 1984.

Thoreau, Henry David. *The Journal of Henry D. Thoreau*. Edited by Bradford Torrey and Francis H. Allen, vols. 1–14, 1837–1861. New York: Dover Publications, 1962.

Twain, Mark. *The Adventures of Huckleberry Finn*. New York: Modern Library, 1968. Originally published 1884.

Twain, Mark. *Following the Equator*, vol. 2. New York: P. F. Collier & Son, Co., 1899.

Tyning, Thomas F. *A Guide to Amphibians and Reptiles*, edited by Donald W. and Lillian Q. Stokes. Stokes Field Guide Series. Boston: Little, Brown and Co., 1990.

Walls, Gordon Lynn. *The Vertebrate Eye and Its Adaptive Radiation*. New York: Hafner, 1963.

Weidensaul, Scott. *Snakes of the World*. Secaucus, NJ: Quintet Publishing Ltd., 1991.

Weidensaul, Scott. "The Belled Viper." *Smithsonian*, 28:9 (December 1997), pp. 96–110.

Wilson, Edward O. "The Serpent," in *Biophilia*. Cambridge, MA: Harvard University Press, 1984.

Wilson, Edward O. *Naturalist*. New York: Warner Books, 1995.

Wright, Albert H., and Anna A. Wright. *Handbook of Snakes*, vols. I and II. Ithaca, NY: Comstock Publishing Associates, 1957.

"Zoo Poisonous Animals Destroyed." *London Times* (Sept. 4, 1939): p. 6.

Zweifel, Richard G. "Alternating Use of Hemipenes in the Kingsnake, *Lampropeltis getula*." *Journal of Herpetology*, 31:3 (1997): pp. 459–461.

Index

About the Author and Photographer

John Netherton, left, and David Badger (Photograph ©Rob Hoffman)

David Badger lives in Franklin, Tennessee, with his wife, Sherry, and son, Jeff. He is professor of journalism at Middle Tennessee State University, where he teaches feature writing, magazine writing, arts reviewing, and motion picture history. He is a former film critic for WPLN-FM Public Radio in Nashville, and a former book critic and columnist for the Nashville *Tennessean*. He grew up in Wilmette, Illinois, and received his A.B. degree from Duke University, M.S.J. degree from Northwestern University, and Ph.D. from the University of Tennessee. He is the author of *Frogs* (Voyageur Press, 1995), with photographs by John Netherton, and *Celebrate the First Amendment*; co-author of *Newscraft*; a contributor to *Free Expression and the American Public*; and the editor of seven books.

John Netherton, a nature photographer for more than thirty years, lives in Nashville, Tennessee, and is the father of three sons, Jason, Joshua, and Erich. His work has appeared in *Audubon, Natural History, National Wildlife, Nikon World, Popular Photography, Birder's World*, and *WildBird*, and he writes a regular column for *Outdoor Photographer*. His books include *Radnor Lake: Nashville's Walden; A Guide to Photography and the Smoky Mountains; Florida: A Guide to Nature and Photography; Tennessee: A Homecoming; Big South Fork Country* (with Senator Howard Baker); *At the Water's Edge: Wading Birds of North America; Tennessee Wonders: A Pictorial Guide to the Parks; Of Breath and Earth: A Book of Days; Frogs* (with David Badger); and *Tennessee: A Bicentennial Celebration*.